In ARDEN

In ARDEN

A Memoir of Four Years
in Shillong, 1974–78

Introduced by Anjum Hasan
Foreword by Easterine Kire *& Afterword by* Paul Pimomo

BRIJRAJ SINGH

Pippa Rann
books & media

Pippa Rann
books & media

An imprint of
Salt Desert Media Group Limited,
7 Mulgrave Chambers, 26 Mulgrave Rd,
Sutton SM2 6LE, England, UK.
Email: pubisher@pipparannbooks.com
Website: www.pipparannbooks.com

Cover picture by Banshimbor1994
distributed under a CC BY-SA 4.0 licence

Inside photographs © Anjum Hasan and Dolcy Suting Melville

ISBN 978-19-13738-73-0

Designed and typeset by Raghav Khattar

Printed and bound at Replika Press Pvt. Ltd, India

MIX
Paper from
responsible sources
FSC® C016779

This book is dedicated
With Great Affection

To All
Who Call the Khasi Hills Home

Duke Senior: And this our life exempt from public haunt
               Finds tongues in trees, books in the
               running brooks,
               Sermons in stones and good in every thing.
                                   As You Like It, II. 1.15-17.

Rosalind: Well, this is the forest of Arden.
Touchstone: Ay, now I am in Arden; the more fool I;
               When I was at home I was in a better place.
                                   As You Like It, II.4.15-17.

CONTENTS

Foreword

In Arden is an easy read, written in a conversational style, bordering even on the confessional in some parts. For everyone who has perhaps never even thought of visiting Shillong, this book is a fascinating introduction to the place at that particular time. For everyone who has lived in Shillong during the 1970s, there will be the pleasure of recollecting the beautifully kept cottages and charming houses with roses climbing along the fencing or fringing the entrance to a home; the sprawling Bara Bazar, loud and vibrant, with its constant movement and noise; the crammed city buses; and Don Bosco square crawling with students at almost every hour of the day. Familiar place names like Laitumkrah, Nongthymmai, Police Bazar, the Shillong Club, La Chaumiere, Ward's lake, Raj Bhavan, and Polo Ground pop up, and crowd the reader's memory with images from the past. I looked forward to each chapter because they were peopled with folk that I had either met or heard of during my student days in Shillong.

So, for the title of the book, why "Arden"? Well, the forest of Arden was the setting for the Shakespearean comedy, 'As you Like it.' It was a semi-magical pastoral location. All who entered the forest had a change of heart, for the better. The house that the Singhs moved into was aptly named Arden, for the journey to the hill station with its fresh air, unpolluted skies and beautiful nature, and not least, the promise of a reduced mosquito population, was truly in the spirit of the romantic tradition.

The Seventies in Shillong was still an era that reflected the cosmopolitan nature of the city with its Chinese, Tibetan, Nepali, Punjabi, Bengali, Naga, Mizo, Sikh, Tamil communities living in the sectors they favoured most, working at trades they found best suited to them. To add to that eclectic mix, Brijraj Singh reminisces about an Armenian family (the Thoroses), an Irishman (Brother Brendan McCartheigh), the Austrian Mrs Ellie Duara, and individuals of other nationalities who made Shillong their home. The magnetism of the hill town was such that it even drew visitors such as anthropologist Christopher von Führer Haimendorf, and world travellers Tom and Jan Conway. Even in that remote past, colleges in Shillong attracted students from Thailand and Bhutan. It was to this charming town (for Shillong was more a town than a city) with its smiling, friendly populace, that Brijraj and his wife Frances travelled to join the new university as teachers.

The book is also an eye-opening perspective on the life of the young university which was set up with high sounding and noble objectives, promising to serve the people of the region but failed to attain that ideal. Brijraj's memoir Is very different from a dry official record. He is very frank about the drawbacks that hindered the university from progressing as it had vowed to. I foresee that he will tread on some toes in his account of the roles played by certain people who failed to take the institution forward. It is important to remember that this is a memoir, and to recognise the right of the writer to render his account in the manner that he experienced it, the right to record his gaze in his way. He does give due warning about this in his introduction by comparing it to one of his earlier books: 'In *Professing English* I gave fictitious names to certain individuals to protect their identity. But here all gloves are off. Everybody is named, friend or foe.' He makes clear in the introduction that the first chapters are light while the following chapters are dark, and 'it was intended to be that way.'

Yet for all that, the writer does not neglect to write in glowing terms about the local people who impressed him with their honesty. He gives the example of the passengers travelling on the very crowded city buses who got off the bus at their stop but always waited to pay their fares instead of slipping away without paying. The Shillong of Brijraj cannot help coming across as animated and ebullient and peopled with 'an uncommonly large number of odd-bods, cranks, eccentrics and otherwise colourful personalities.' He adds, 'We got to know several and loved them all.' His description of people they came to know is generous. Mr Booth, their landlord is described as 'a prince among men.' He remembers fondly the kindness of Nari Rustomji and his family, as well as the Duaras and their local neighbours at Arden, all trying to welcome newcomers to the town they loved.

Brijraj and Frances left Shillong in 1978, but they carried a part of it with them in the person of their *kong*, Dolcy, who accompanied them first to Delhi, and then to the US as a member of their family, and continues to stay in their lives even after she has married and moved out to a relatively remote place far from them in USA.

For a reader, there is much to take away from a book like this. I find value in the bits of historical information on Shillong and its people that salt the narrative. In places like the Northeast where many community histories exist only in the form of official records, memoirs have an important role to play. They offer a window into a particular period in history, containing information that can't be found elsewhere except in people's memories. *In Arden* is important for its own sake as well as for the sake of what it brings to the table of community history.

– **Easterine Kire**

Introduction

SHILLONG COULD SEEM LIKE A GIFT OF DESTINY TO many people who migrated there in the decades after Indian independence. This small but significant capital city or large but sleepy hill town – it can be both at the same time – has tended to excite the imagination of its more educated settlers. Its uncommonly diverse population created over time a unique even if not consistently robust urban culture. With the British colonials came soldiers, tradesmen, clerks, educators and tea planters from all over India; the Bengali bhadralok treated it as an outpost of Calcutta and Sylhet, some attempting a renaissance-inspired programme of social reform; after 1947 the Assamese ran the region's administration from here; and then, once Shillong became the capital of Meghalaya in 1972, more immigrants followed in measured doses, some working at institutions set up to further the goal – then as now treated with ambivalence – of ushering the region into the so-called national mainstream.

Set up in the mid-1970s, the North Eastern Hill University was one such place. This book is the story of Brijraj and Frances Singh's years at NEHU and provides an invaluable personal account of just this ambivalence, invaluable because it is so rare to read of Shillong as an experience rather than just a setting for history or politics. There is the excitement of institution-building in uncharted waters, the enormous charm of Shillong's landscape and its gallery of intriguing locals and, eventually, the pettiness and provincialism that can wear one out. Brij sees a higher purpose in coming to Shillong and arrives eager to put into practice new ideas about teaching English. But the disappointments that follow also show that Shillong did not and perhaps can never fulfil its potential as an arcadia – that despite the charming hodgepodge of its cosmopolitanism, the underlying anxieties besetting both native and outsider tend to get the upper hand. These violent contradictions between being a forward-looking modern city and a secure tribal homeland were starting to show in the '70s and have only become more pronounced with time; and Brij unerringly puts his finger on the problem.

Brij's close friend and my father, Noorul Hasan, who appears in the narrative, made a similar move from Delhi to Shillong before I was born, to become part of the same dream that produced NEHU. He suffered many of the same frustrations and upsets that Brij recounts. Unlike Brij who returned to Delhi and then left India, my father remained in Shillong, and those early, pioneering years acquired in his memory – and in the stories he told my siblings and I – the quality of a myth. To learn now from Brij's account that the myth was peopled by all too human creatures, prone to both great visions and serious failings, is educative.

But in one respect both Brij and Noorul's sense of value and understanding of their place in the world was and is derived from the same thing – the reading, the writing and, above all, the teaching of English literature. Shillong in this book is both enchanted forest and fool's paradise. To be able to see this, to illuminate the bind through metaphor, is how literature makes it possible to inhabit the world. And so *In Arden* is a paean to two kinds of loves and two kinds of losses: literature and Shillong; the private consolations of literature that cannot always compensate for public politicking; and the city of the imagination that does not always measure up to the city riding roughshod out on the street.

– Anjum Hasan, Bangalore, December 2020

PREFACE

MY WIFE FRANCES AND I LIVED AND WORKED IN Shillong for four years, from 1974 to 1978. Our myriad experiences there made a powerful impression on both of us, and I began planning this book on the train the day I left Shillong to return to Delhi. Frances joined me the following month, and shortly afterwards I started writing what I had planned. I wrote by hand at white heat in notebooks bought from Delhi's Super Bazar. Words just tumbled out, and in a couple of months or so I had finished the first five chapters. Then I hit a block. I just couldn't start the next chapter that was going to be about working at the North-Eastern Hill University (NEHU) in Shillong. The experiences were too raw, too painful, too recent; certain things still rankled, and I could not develop the kind of distance necessary to write reasonably objectively and fairly. So I stopped writing and the notebooks just lay on a neglected corner of my desk.

In 2009 I wrote my teaching memoirs with the title *Professing English on Two Continents*. One of the chapters was going to be on my years of teaching at

NEHU. By now my bitterness and pain had become ancient history. Though after all those years I was not able to remember all the details with the same immediacy and vividness with which I had written the other chapters on Shillong, I was able to string together enough to make for a respectable chapter.

Recently some of my nieces asked me to write vignettes of my early life so that they and their children would get to know me better; and that impelled me to open the notebooks again to see what I had written about Shillong in 1978. As I read those pages, forgotten or half buried memories came alive again, and I decided that perhaps those pages were worth saving. So I sat down at my computer and word processed what I had written, and then, deciding that it was finally time to finish the book, went back to *Professing English* to familiarize myself with what I had said about NEHU. I found that by using that chapter as a foundation, and adding some more details and a longer discussion of certain people and topics, I could produce a reasonably objective account (though from my point of view) of the university without concealing any wounds or bitterness that I felt while there. In *Professing English*, I gave fictitious names to certain individuals to protect their identity. But here all gloves are off. Everybody is named, friend or foe.

So the book has been completed at last, and I offer it to the reader as an account of what things were like in Meghalaya and NEHU nearly fifty years ago, and how two people in their late twenties and early thirties saw them. Much has changed since then. I have been back to Shillong only once since I left in 1978. That was in 1990 when Frances and I spent a week with our friend Noorul Hasan on the new NEHU campus. Already there was change everywhere. There was far more traffic and more tall buildings made of cement and concrete than in the 1970s. I am sure that were I to go back again today, I would not be able to recognize much of Shillong. This is probably where the value of the book lies. For it gives people today a sense of what things were like in the past, and therefore a helpful and accurate yardstick for judging how far they have come. And it gives anyone interested in the history of NEHU some glimpses into its earliest years.

In any case, though the external lineaments of a society or culture may undergo rapid changes, its essential nature, its sense of itself, changes much more slowly. More women in the Khasi Hills today may prefer jeans to the traditional *jainsem*, more men and women may travel to other parts of the country or work there, there may be a greater awareness of local artists at work, whether in the field of music or dance or literature, and there is certainly much more creativity among the Khasis today than when I lived there. Shillong has produced musicians and film makers who have made a name for themselves nationally, even internationally. People in the Khasi

Hills have become trendsetters for the rest of India in various ways.

Another important change is worth noting. In Chapter 3 ("Friends") I offer some rather uncharitable remarks about the provincialism and insularity of some professional middle class Khasis that we noticed when we lived there. There is no question but that today those attitudes have dissipated. I am quite sure that the professional middle-class Khasi today is just as cultivated, urbane and interesting as any other Indian of his or her class, and had we been living there now, we should have made many friends from that class.

But many of the basic aspects of Khasi society, some of whose essential features I try to capture in this book, have not changed all that much in several respects. Several old ways of doing certain things are still in use. Old values remain the bedrock of the Khasi world. So the reader can use this book to study the extent to which Khasi society has remained more or less the same while the external features of life have undergone tremendous changes.

In the last chapter, "Respice," I bring the story up to date as far as my knowledge allows.

Even when I wrote most of this book in 1978, I was aware that it fell into two parts. The early chapters were light and expressed the excitement that two young people felt at coming to a new place and making a home there. Some of this tone continued into the third chapter, but already there were intimations that now we had started being more analytical and more critical about our experiences. The fourth and fifth chapters are much more in the nature of an investigative report about the place we inhabited and the people we encountered, and describe not so much our experiences as what we had learned. Finally, something of the personal tone returns in the sixth chapter, but things are altogether less happy, more dark. The change between the beginning and the end is perceptible. It was intended to be that way.

One final word. The prices quoted in this book are those that prevailed fifty years ago. Certain names and spellings, like Gauhati, Bombay and Madras, that were current then, have been retained. But I am aware that today they are Guwahati, Mumbai and Chennai.

– **Brijraj Singh,**
Delhi, 1978; New York, 2009, 2020

Chapter 1
GETTING THERE

Ultimately, I suppose, we decided to leave Delhi for Shillong just because June 1974, when I was offered a job in the new North-Eastern Hill University (hereafter NEHU), was beastly hot, as all Junes are in Delhi, while Shillong is a hill station. Besides, Shillong sounded exciting and exotic, and the new university promised opportunities for innovation, trying out new ideas, and, finally, promotion. To go to Shillong seemed an adventure, and my wife and I love adventures.

Just how exotic Shillong seemed from Delhi became clear a few days later when I went to my bank to have my account transferred.

"Ah yes, Ceylon," said the Manager. "Have you got your passports already?"

I informed him that it was Shillong, not Ceylon.

"You must forgive my pronunciation," he said. "I understand that it is very hot there all through the year."

"On the contrary," I replied, "it's supposed to be

cool. That's why we are going."

"Really? But it's almost on the Equator."

By now the clerks, always on the lookout for an argument or discussion, which they find so much more interesting than the work they are paid to do, had stopped working and were listening eagerly. One bright young man, probably fresh to the bank from college, joined the discussion at this point, obviously relishing the chance of upstaging the Manager.

"Of course Shillong isn't on the Equator. That's Ceylon. Shillong is in India, in Assam."

"Well, actually," I said, "it used to be in Assam but isn't so any more now. It's in Meghalaya."

"Meghalaya! Where's Meghalaya?" another clerk joined in.

By now several people were talking at the same time.

"Meghalaya is in Assam." "Isn't that Nagaland?" "I had a cousin in Gauhati once. He said milk was very cheap there." "Is that where they eat rats?" "Who's taking the flat you are vacating?" This last one from a customer.

The young woman who wrote my new address down was thoroughly confused by now. "North Eastern Hill University, Shillong, Meghaland," she entered in her book. If my bank hasn't done anything else, it has at least given India a new State.

Muriel Wasi is an elderly lady of the most unimpeachable integrity of character, a hard, at times aggressive exterior, and a great concern, even tenderness, for people, especially the young, in her heart. My wife and I admire her immensely.

"Mrs. Wasi," I told her, "we have a bit of news for you. We are leaving Delhi for Shillong, where I have accepted a post at NEHU."

"Nay who?" she answered, "neigh hoo? What is that?" And before I could reply, she added, "Sounds like an ass braying. Are you sure you'll like it, whatever it is?"

We laughed then. We should have known that wisdom has many guises, and off-hand, dismissive comments can be one of them.

Actually, we'd stopped off at Mrs. Wasi's on our way to the India International Centre. The Vice Chancellor of NEHU was staying there on a visit to Delhi, and wanted to see me to find out, no doubt, what kind of a person he had recruited. I was equally keen on meeting him to find out what kind of a boss I was getting.

I had met CDS Devanesen briefly several years ago when he was Principal of the Madras Christian College. He had made little impression on me then. Since he had taken over as the Vice Chancellor of NEHU, however, I had heard a good deal about him, all very encouraging. NEHU was to be the brave new academic world of the future, and he, like Moses, was to lead us to it.

No one could have looked less like Moses than Devanesen as he greeted us in the India International

Centre. Dark, short, with silvery hair brushed back and blood-shot eyes, wearing a dark blue bush shirt and pants of a dark, rather nondescript color, he didn't look like my idea of a dynamic, forward-looking Vice Chancellor at all—at least, not till he began to speak. Then I was simply swept off my feet by his charm, his warm friendliness, unaffected good humor, and his magnificent vision of the new university which he had been chosen to head. Listening to him I got the impression that I was in the presence of a visionary who was also a man of action, so full was he of the need, in NEHU, to be innovative, creative, experimental all the time, of the marvelous world of the tribals whom the university was going to serve, of the new courses we would be required to devise, the new library we would have to build up, and of how he was working towards this ideal day and night, frequently consulting the Union Education Minister, all the time with the University Grants Commission, and always darting off to Nagaland or Mizoram to discuss the educational needs of the people there. He seemed to me to be an absolute dynamo of energy, a man who had had a dream and was determined to realize it.

"And it should be possible for Frances to get a job in NEHU also," he concluded.

My cup of joy ran over. Here was I, chosen to be part of a team that was going to show a skeptical nation that Indian universities **could** work efficiently, and that they had a genuine contribution to make to the community. This team was going to be directed in its work by a most outstanding leader. And now he was inviting my wife to join in this marvelous adventure! What more could I ask for?

Just one bit of information.

"How much will I be paid?" I asked.

A look of distaste came into the Vice Chancellor's eyes. They seemed to say that these were mundane matters with which he couldn't be concerned. But his tone remained friendly, cheerful, even airy.

"Oh, well, no doubt you'll get a handsome starting salary. It is not my principle to start people off on a low salary when we can afford to give them more. Also, I know for a fact that you'll be entitled to a house rent allowance of rupees 450. But these are such trifling details! Surely we have more important things to think about than money. Indeed, I have never shown much respect for it myself. In Madras I had an excellent Bursar who managed college finances; and I have made it a rule that if you don't think about money too much, you are freer to get on with the things that really count."

I was suitably abashed. How could I be so crass, I wondered. I hoped that the Vice Chancellor (VC hereafter) hadn't misunderstood the purpose of my question—I hoped he didn't think I was an opportunist!

Frances, in the meanwhile, had a question too. "Are there any mosquitoes in Shillong, Dr Devanesen?" she inquired.

Her question took Devanesen aback. It didn't me, for I knew the background. Frances has a remarkable knack, when in a room, for attracting all the mosquitoes present to herself, just as she was to show great talent later, in the forests of Meghalaya and Assam, for attracting all the leeches present. I cannot explain this over-fondness of a certain type of God's creation for her, nor, truth to tell, have I ever been jealous. On the contrary, it has been my experience, since I married her, to have received remarkably few mosquito bites, all the mosquitoes at night obviously possessing a preference for the taste of her blood. I have sometimes jokingly referred to her as my best insurance against malaria, but I sympathize with her too as she tosses and turns in bed on hot nights and slaps various parts of her anatomy in a vain attempt to get even with her persecutors. So I listened to the VC's answer with interest.

He quickly regained his composure. "Oh no!" he replied laughing. "There are no mosquitoes in Shillong. The place is much too high for them to fly up to."

The answer relieved Frances. However, when, at the end of our meeting with Devanesen, we compared notes, I found her less enthusiastic about my boss-to-be than I was.

"But what did you not like about him?" I pressed her. "I think he's absolutely charming and knows exactly what he wants. In fact, I think it's going to be great working with him."

"Well," she said, "he's going to be your boss, not mine. But I don't like people who talk too much about themselves. Besides, he sounds vague on money matters."

"That's because he is an idealist," I said. "Unlike you," I wanted to add, but refrained.

"Well," said Frances, "I'd rather take a man who was sound on finances and short on ideals."

Her attempt at a slick, cynical aphorism displeased me somewhat. She is a New Yorker, and not easily impressed. Which is fine, I've always thought, except that it comes close, at times, to a point of view which is downright materialistic. Cynicism and worldly wisdom are ok in their place, but surely there are times when one has to be responsive to ideals, and believe in values greater than the self. No, there is no question but that I felt ticked off by Frances.

One of my weak points, I have now begun to discern, is that I tend to over-value reason and idealism and do not always recognize the greater claims of feminine intuition. This lesson has come to me largely through working at NEHU for four years Shillong taught me many things. One of them was that my rent allowance was not 450 rupees but only 375, less 10% of my salary. Another was that there **are** mosquitoes in Shillong.

We were at the New Delhi railway station. Frances had used up three cans of rather expensive paint in getting fourteen pieces of our luggage to inform those whom it might concern, or who might just be curious, that they belonged to B. Singh, and were bound from New Delhi to Gauhati, and thence to Shillong. When the fourteen pieces were weighed, they also announced their combined *avoir dupois* as totaling seven quintals. Four of these seven were our books; and just over a kilo represented another prized possession, drugged for the occasion and curled up in his wicker basket: Cat.

Cat had walked into a classroom nine months previously and walked straight into our lives and our hearts. He was black, but the reason we called him Othello was because he had green eyes. Rather, that was his name when he was still small enough to climb into my jacket pocket in search of warmth. As he grew older he realized what any cat, according to T. S. Eliot, finds out sooner or later. He had to have more names. So when he began to worship the refrigerator as the source of all good things, we christened him Kelvinator, and later, when he discovered one day where the pudding was kept, Pudding, which I pronounced "Monster." But the name that he liked to contemplate best in his ineffably effable way was Cat, a word that we discovered was capable of a surprisingly remarkable range of inflections, and therefore meanings. *Cat* means anger, desperation, frustration, cuddliness, furriness, happiness, and a host of other emotions, severally or collectively, depending on how you say the word.

How Cat was to be transported to Shillong had given us some anxious moments. After several deliberations we decided to consult a vet, who said that animals were best transported under sedation. He recommended a tranquilizer, and said that two teaspoons would be enough.

Three nights before we were to leave, I decided to make sure that the vet's advice was sound, and gave Cat the prescribed two spoonsful. But Cat was a healthy, vigorous animal, and all through the night kept bounding up and down as was his wont, supremely indifferent to the effect the tranquilizer was supposed to have. This made Frances and me rather apprehensive, and so the next night we gave him four teaspoons. Cat looked at us with hurt, accusing eyes, went into a corner, licked the remnants of the medicine off his whiskers, and went out for a post-prandial perambulation. He returned some hours afterwards, and spent the rest of the night chasing imaginary mice.

We were truly alarmed. The next night was to be our last in Delhi, and if we couldn't get Monster sedated, we wouldn't know what to do with him once we boarded the train. It was do or die, and so that night I poured half the bottle down his unwilling throat. The vet would have been shocked, but desperate men need desperate remedies. This time the medicine worked. In less than half an hour Cat had fallen into a deep, limp sleep. It was in this condition that he was shut into his basket and put on the train. His sleep lasted

24 hours till we were in Barauni. At the first signs of returning consciousness, I transferred what remained in the bottle into the animal, and he went off to sleep again. Hereafter he was completely oblivious to the excitements and rigors of the long journey, and awakened only when we were safely ensconced in a room in the Legislative Assembly hostel in Shillong. If he felt any puzzlement or wonder at his new surroundings, he kept his feelings to himself.

Notwithstanding his rather undignified mode of travel, my guess is that Cat enjoyed his journey rather more than Frances and I did. The start from Delhi had been auspicious enough. So many of our friends had come to the station to see us off that we did not feel we were leaving like refugees. The luggage had been loaded properly under my supervision. "Please make sure the fridge is carried upright," Frances had instructed me, and I had fulfilled this command to the letter, though it had cost me the goodwill of the porters and an extra ten rupees as tips. The train had started on time, we were the only occupants of our compartment, and the sandwiches we had brought along for lunch were superb. "How has it gone so far?" I asked Frances; and she smiled and said, "So far, so good."

We didn't have to go too much further before it became not so good. To be precise, Barauni marked the turning point.

Barauni, in Bihar, is a station that has long been familiar to travelers to and from north-east India, and it is always dreaded by them as a place where anything can happen, and usually does. In our four years in Shillong we were to hear many hair-raising experiences of Khasis and others who had been through there. Muddles over reservations, missed trains, stolen luggage, lost children, and fainting in the heat would seem, from these stories, to be common run-of-the-mill occurrences. To these stories we can add some more.

Our train reached Barauni on time, at 4 o'clock in the morning. The meter gauge train which we were now to take for Gauhati would not leave till 7, so we had three clear hours in which to find the compartment that would be our home for the next twenty-four hours, and have our heavy luggage shifted from the brake van of the broad gauge to that of the meter gauge train. We decided on a plan of action. I would take Frances and Cat to the compartment which had been reserved for us, and then, after ensconcing them there with our lighter luggage, lend moral—and a bit of material—support to the porters who were responsible for transferring the heavy luggage from one brake van to the other. I found the porters, chatted them up, waved a ten-rupee note vaguely in the air, and asked them if they were going to engage in the task for which the Indian Railways paid them. Tomorrow, they replied, would be soon enough. Would not today do just as well? I asked. It could, they seemed to think, except that the government paid them so little that they saw no reason for doing today what they could put off till tomorrow. I waved another five-rupee note in the air. Suppose, I suggested, somebody were to help the government in its hallowed task of paying them, could things be speeded up somewhat? They could, indeed, they replied, but where were the generous souls who could add a full twenty rupees to what the government paid them every month? I took the hint. What they were asking for was a bit excessive, but I needed their services, and needed them now. Beggars can't be choosers, I said to myself; and though the porters' demands seemed directed towards making me take a small step in that direction, the bank would not break altogether if I waved yet another five-rupee note. Rather reluctantly, therefore, I did so. The result was instantaneous. With shouted cautions and much heaving, our luggage began to be transferred from one train to the other at an altogether satisfactory speed.

Since the two brake vans were at diagonally opposite ends of a platform, I got plenty of exercise that morning in walking up and down it, with load-carrying porters in tow. I noticed, in the course of one such crossing, an emaciated man begging for alms. On the fourth or fifth crossing I noticed a small ring of people surrounding an object on the floor. Normally I should have hurried on my business, but since the ring was directly in my way I paused to look. There was the beggar lying dead, and flies were already beginning to settle on him.

It is impossible to describe how I felt then, or have done so often since, when recalling the scene. Appalled horror, uncomprehending shock, great anger: I felt them all, and yet none of these words really gets to the truth. It was obvious that the beggar had collapsed due to years of disease and malnutrition. That such a thing was possible, that it could happen in a big railway station, and that there was nothing one could do for him, and for countless others like him, were thoughts that flashed through my mind in a second. I felt small and ashamed when I thought that if he had accosted me just ten minutes ago, I should probably have given him a twenty-paise coin and not thought about the matter twice. But suppose I had known, even as I was giving him alms, that only a little bit later he would collapse and die—ah, what then? What would I have done? Would I have bought him a meal? Or given him all the money I had? Missed my train and rushed him to the hospital? Reported to the station master? Called the police? I didn't know. And even as I knew that I didn't know, I knew, too, that none of these things would have helped. One timid gesture, or even a grand gesture, does not make up for years of neglect, and oppression, and wrong. And yet in what way could I, as an individual, be held responsible for what had happened? I stood in the ring, confused and baffled and deeply sorry and angry at the same time, till the police came, covered up the corpse, and shooed us away. It was in a chastened, subdued and shocked manner that I made my last trip across the platform, this time trailing behind the porters and forcing myself to take one step after another.

I had decided that I would not tell Frances anything about it or else she, too, would get needlessly worked up. But as soon as I came up to her, I knew something was wrong. She wasn't crying any more, but looked upset. "What's the matter?" I asked, apprehensively. At first she wouldn't tell; like me, she, too, was hoarding up her unpleasant secret less it should cause me pain. But finally I coaxed it out of her.

A few soldiers had passed by her carriage window and, seeing an unaccompanied young woman, had decided to make advances. First they had tried to hold a conversation in broken English; but when she had snubbed them, one of them had produced a bottle of rum and tried to force it down between her lips. Frances had, quite properly, screamed, pulled down the shutters and bolted the door. But she was upset. The closed compartment was hot, stuffy and dark, but there she had sat till she saw me coming.

Again, what could I do? The soldiers had disappeared, and it seemed the only sensible thing to do was to cheer Frances up and make her see the absurdity of the situation. This I succeeded in doing after some time. "After all," I concluded, "this is Barauni, and in Barauni anything can happen. Remember?" She smiled, and once the train started her cheerfulness returned.

I was more somber. She questioned me, trying to find out if anything was wrong; then, suspecting that I was upset on account of her misadventure, told me not to think of it any more, as she, too, had stopped minding. But, though I did not tell her this then, it was not her experience that was troubling me. I was thinking of the beggar.

If I were a poet or philosopher I might have been able to relate the two experiences, and, using them as a starting point, perhaps probe a truth about human life. I might have been able to offer a statement or a testament. As it was, the only relations I could establish were superficial, and my only conclusions trite or portentous. They ran something like this: sex and death are the only realities. Again, it is symptomatic of India and perhaps of the world today that while on the one hand there has been a breakdown of respect, ceremony, innocence, on the other we have failed to provide even for physical well-being. Materialism cannot guarantee even itself. And then I went round again to the same point by reflecting that all life except one's own had ceased to matter and even a selfish, individual life was not possible for many.

In the meanwhile, the train ran on through Bihar which grew hotter as the day wore on. Wherever you looked out of the window you saw water, for Bihar was in the grip of one of its usual calamities. It was the floods that had probably driven the beggar from some remote village to a big and bustling railway junction, there to meet a meaningless end. No crops were visible anywhere. Sometimes the flood waters were only feet away from the railway tracks; and when that happened, the train slowed down. By the time we reached Katihar we were running two hours late. At Siliguri we were four hours behind schedule. Each of the wayside stations was crowded by hordes of half-naked villagers from their engulfed villages, the men smoking, staring, spitting, the women despairing. And there were children everywhere, too weak to run about and play and shout, but defecating everywhere. Their mothers didn't mind. They cleaned them, and continued to stare despairingly. The villages, when they could be seen from the train, were generally only partially visible: a few thatched rooftops sticking out of the water, the odd electric pole half-submerged. Such people as we saw in the countryside were in boats, or sitting upon railway embankments. Most of them seemed to have congregated at railway stations, there to await the receding of the floods. Perhaps the government and private agencies were feeding them and inoculating them against disease. But we never found out. Whenever the train stopped, a few emaciated hands would be thrust through the window into the carriage, and we gave what we could. But to give a coin to one meant inviting a hundred demanding more, and our resources were limited. Sympathy was not needed, and it would not have been understood. Only food and money was demanded; and when it was not forthcoming, there came into these hundreds of eyes a look that was neither anger nor hostility nor self-pity. It was a look that said that they understood because you had seen through them. For the truth is that when someone coaxed a coin out of you, the look in his or her eye was likely to be not one of gratitude but rather that of a cunning, sly craftiness. "Ah ha, I've fooled you!" it seemed to say, The next worst thing to shutting one's eyes to poverty, I decided, was to idealize and sentimentalize it.

By Siliguri it was dark, and we went to bed. I woke up once, around midnight it must have been, to find we were still in Siliguri. When, or whether, we passed through Naxalbari I do not know. I do know that when we woke up, we were not too far from Gauhati, and the landscape had changed beyond recognition.

There was still water everywhere, but it was no longer an alien element covering everything, shapeless and destructive. Not that it was now channeled and controlled, but there seemed to be a reason and a purpose to it. It was let into paddy fields through small cuts in embankments, men, women and children could be seen at every place sitting by it with rod in hand, or else flinging fishing nets into it, and boats carried people to known and intended destinations over it. It wasn't something to flee from, neither was it a tamed, decorated pet. It retained its elementally, and the people theirs, and men and water lived side by side on terms of familiarity and respect. Little, rickety and really quite picturesque bamboo bridges were flung over it to connect villages to fields, and sometimes even one house in a village to another. The villages themselves were made up of little clusters of palm-thatched huts set on dry land in little clearings. Where there was land, but no huts, there was thick, lush, tropical vegetation. We recognized bananas, but what were all these other broad-leafed trees? The sky was blue, with a few fleeting clouds, and the air washed and pure. Surely this was an idyll, I thought, till my experiences in Bihar the day before made me realize with greater force than might otherwise have been possible that the people who lived in these Assam villages wouldn't thank me for sentimentalizing and idealizing their condition. Growing paddy is hard work, and the cereal itself does not provide the nutrition and strength necessary for this kind of work. Besides, working in paddy fields means leeches and snakes all the time. Fish is small, and the methods of fishing primitive. And malaria and gastric parasites are eternal, unwelcome guests in the human system. No, I was determined I would not glamorize poverty any more, but see it for the harsh evil it is.

Looking back, I wonder if I wasn't wrong. If I would not want to change places with the villager, would he necessarily want to change places with me? His life might be wretched and poor, but it was his life after all, and it offered him just as much or little happiness as the lives of others offer them. If I would be wrong in sensing my life as being better, would I not be equally wrong in raging because his life was no better? But I didn't have time for further puerile thoughts just then, for the train started making the peculiar rattling noise that it makes when it goes over bridges, and there was the Brahmaputra, vast, fast flowing and muddy beneath me, and shortly afterwards we pulled into Gauhati. I gave Frances a reassuring squeeze because we had just completed the first stage of our adventures, or preliminaries, as it were, and were about to step into the real thing. And I stepped out on to the platform and literally into a pile of shit.

The Vice Chancellor had promised, when we met him in Delhi, to send a university jeep to meet us at Gauhati station, but he had also said that if no university transport were available, we were to make our own way up to Shillong. Therefore, when I had walked up and down the platform two or three times without encountering any NEHU representative, I assumed that no one had come to meet us, and therefore had our luggage unloaded from the train and carried across the track to the other side of the station from where buses and taxis were available for the three-hour, hundred-kilometer long road journey to Shillong. Since we had rather a lot of luggage, we thought that it would be best to hire a taxi which could accommodate not only ourselves and Cat but also our suitcases containing our clothes, while the heavy luggage could be booked to follow us the next day by an Assam Government Roadways truck. By now Frances was beginning to feel rather tired and nauseous, and so though it was lunchtime, we thought it best to set off without delay and stop over on the way somewhere for a quick lunch. By 2:30 p.m. all arrangements were made, and we clambered into the taxi over piles of luggage.

It takes a great deal of doing to unnerve taxi drivers, but ours looked visibly shaken after Cat, from within his basket, had let out a few drowsy sounds. We assured the man that it was only a cat; and when he found we were animal lovers, became talkative. We let him talk, since we were eager to get as much information about Shillong as possible before we actually got there.

What our driver told us wasn't very encouraging. Everything was expensive, good vegetables unobtainable for the better part of the year, housing difficult. Of course, I was willing to make allowances for the fact that our informant was definitely prejudiced. He was Assamese, and we knew that Meghalaya had been carved out of Assam not long ago because the hill people had resented the way the Assamese, who controlled politics and money, had either exploited the tribals or else ignored them altogether, sinking massive development funds into the villages and cities of the Brahmaputra valley and doing hardly anything to help the development of the hill areas. Assam had had to pay for its callous shortsightedness; and now, having lost Meghalaya and other hill areas, could only vent its impotent rage through calumny directed at the new hill States. So we listened to our taxi driver with growing amusement and disbelief, especially when he decried the Khasis for being beef eaters and their women for being what sounded to my ear as yet unused to Assamese pronunciation as "lauje." Curious, I asked him what that meant. He gave me a look of withering scorn and answered, "Lauje women are seep." This interested me. I had heard several things about Khasi women, all of them complimentary, but never that they were lauje and seep. Besides, I was an English teacher, and here were two words being added to my vocabulary whose meanings I did not know. I pressed him to expound his meaning.

My curiosity, however, had an effect just the opposite to what I had intended. The driver, quite convinced that I was pulling his leg, for how could a man my age not know about loose and cheap women, if only by hearsay, set his eyes firmly on the road and began to concentrate all his attention on warning oncoming traffic of his murderous intentions by blowing his horn loud and long.

This gave us time to observe our surroundings. A friend in Delhi had described the Gauhati-Shillong road, along which he had driven a few years previously, as a well-surfaced dual carriageway. What he meant, I suppose, was that two cars could pass each other without their sides quite touching. Once we started climbing, which we did just about ten miles out of Gauhati, we realized, too, that while there might be worse surfaced roads, there couldn't be too many with so many curves and hairpin bends. I noticed, however, that work on improving the road was in progress in a number of places. When we left Shillong for good after four years the work was still in progress. Hill roads obviously take a long time to repair. In the meanwhile, our driver's methods of propelling the taxi were also aimed at making us slide in our seats from one end to another, so that by the time we got to Nongpoh, exactly halfway between Gauhati and Shillong, I was feeling pretty shattered and Frances was looking rather yellow. As for Cat, we thought it would be best to let sleeping cats lie. while we had some refreshment.

Nongpoh! How many travelers in India's north-eastern States have thrilled to that name. It is here that you stop for your first cup of tea and your first welcome breath of cool mountain air if you are Shillong-bound. It is here that you are first introduced to the glorious fruit of the Khasi hills, and to the absurdly high prices that prevail in this region. It is here that you first set foot on the soil of Meghalaya. And it is here that you have your first close look at the Khasis. I could talk for ever on each of these subjects. But I must first tell you something about the geographical boundaries between Meghalaya and Assam, and Nongpoh is as good a place as any to receive our first introduction to this vexed subject.

When Meghalaya was carved out of Assam in 1972, the exact boundaries between the two States were left undemarcated. Roughly speaking, the Gauhati-Shillong road divides them, so that as you drive up, the fields on the left belong to Assam while the hills on the right are Meghalaya. After about ten or twelve miles Meghalaya starts owning the fields on the left as well: you are now well and truly in the hill State. But because the road turns and twists so much, certain areas that appear from one spot to belong to Assam appear from another point in the road to be Meghalaya's. It is these areas that cause confusion. When, for instance, the Assam government decided to construct a guest house for Mrs. Gandhi when she came to Gauhati to attend the Congress session in 1975, the spot chosen was a small hill just outside Gauhati. The people of Meghalaya protested, saying that the site was in their State, but Assam went ahead nevertheless. Now some people in Meghalaya are claiming the guest house while the present Assam government is charge-sheeting various people associated with the erstwhile Congress government for having squandered money on the project.

Assam, in fact, has been having a lot of difficulty over its borders. Sometime ago the Nagas raided some villages in Assam and killed several people; more recently there was trouble with Arunachal Pradesh. The Assam-Meghalaya border is comparatively quiet, but here, too, from time to time there are cases of cattle lifting from the other side, and sometimes quite bizarre forms of protest. Not long ago a police party from one State dislodged boundary markers near a village to protest against encroachments by the other side in another village.

The area of Meghalaya that lies between Shillong and Gauhati is called Bhoi, and Nongpoh is its sub-divisional headquarters. Many of the inhabitants are Khasis, but there are also a lot of Cachari tribals and Nepalis as well. The Nepalis in particular find themselves in a rather ambivalent and unenviable position. Several of them are recent immigrants and don't hold Indian citizenship. As such, they are not wanted in Meghalaya, where a large section of the population feels that if this kind of immigration is allowed to continue the Khasis, the Garos and the Jaintias, the three tribes of Meghalaya, will eventually be reduced to a minority in their own State. At the same time the Nepalis are indispensable to the economy of the State, since they provide a cheap and ready labor force. The situation has resulted in a lot of human exploitation. In Bhoi, for insance, there is a good deal of arable land, all owned by the Khasis. But these landlords do not cultivate their holdings. They live in Shillong, while the work on the fields is done by Nepali sharecroppers. The families of these sharecroppers live in great filth and poverty, but they cannot do anything to better their lot since these foreign nationals ought not to be there in the first place. The government, too, is more keen to check "outsiders" from coming into the State than in alleviating the condition of those actually there. And because both the Union and State governments are desirous of protecting the rights of the tribals and minorities, and because the Khasis are tribals and a minority community, the powers that be feel that they have done their duty by ensuring that only Khasis can own land in Bhoi. But in Meghalaya, as in other north-eastern States, there is the problem of minorities within minorities; and in protecting the community which is, by all-India standards, a minority (the Khasis), a great deal of injustice is capable of being done to other communities like the Nepalis, for whom the all-India minority community is the dominant majority.

The system of sharecropping is one reason why Bhoi's agriculture is undeveloped. Another is that Bhoi is an unhealthy region. Lying between a few hundred feet above sea level and roughly 2500 feet, and possessing numerous little streams, pools and ponds, the area abounds in mosquitoes. Malaria is not unknown even now; till some years ago it was rife. The fever so debilitated the sufferer that his productivity was drastically reduced. Add to this the fact that, apart from the odd dispensary, proper medical facilities were unknown till recently, and you can understand why Bhoi is one of the most depressed parts of the Khasi hills.

Its great asset is its forests and wild life. You can find wild elephants in the lower reaches of Bhoi, together with leopard, wild boar, python and deer. Our landlord in Shillong, Mr. Booth, who owns a small farm in Bhoi, often told us of the leopard claw marks he frequently found on his trees, and of how a wild elephant had once died in the little stream from which he got his water. The rotting animal polluted the stream, and Mr. Booth was afraid that it was going to be months before he could use it again. But in a week or ten days' time the whole carcase had disappeared, hacked to pieces and carried away as meat by neighboring villagers.

This was a case of an animal dying a natural death. Unfortunately a lot of wanton destruction takes place. The Nepalis and Cacharis kill for food, but several rich and not-so-rich Khasis come and poach also. One Bhoi politician told me proudly that he was happiest when cooking and eating wild boar which he had shot, and he tried to give himself as much of this happiness as he could; only, the government got in his way sometimes with their new-fangled rules for the protection of wild animals. What did God make wild animals for but to be killed, he demanded. Luckily, he went on, most of the people responsible for implementing these laws in Bhoi were his friends and did not grudge him his weekly or fortnightly quota of happiness.

When you reach Nongpoh a sign informs you that the sale of venison is an offense under the law. The intention is obviously to preserve the deer population of Bhoi. I used to be impressed by this sign till I was once served some excellent venison at a friend's house.

"Where did you get it from?" I asked.

"From Nongpoh, of course, "he replied. "That's where you get the best and cheapest venison."

As you drive up to Nongpoh, you notice hundreds of little pineapple plantations on both sides of the road, and unless you have lived with pineapples all your life your most lasting memories of Nongpoh are likely to be of mounds of pineapples and other fruit like bananas, oranges and plums for sale. Of these, only pineapples are locally produced. The oranges come from Dawki on the Bangladesh border, the bananas from Cherrapunji, and the plums from there and from Shillong. The pineapples that you get in July, August and September are cheap, juicy and sweet; those that you get in the winter less so. The other fruit are all delicious but expensive: bananas, for instance, may cost anything between five and eight rupees a dozen. Prices notwithstanding, Nongpoh is the place for fruit, and every bus, car, taxi and jeep that stops here disgorges people who make a beeline for the fruit shops. Fruit from here is eaten in many cities of the country, and if some evening at Palam or Santa Cruz airport you see passengers carrying a couple of pineapples, you can be certain that they were bought earlier that day in Nongpoh.

You know, when you reach Nongpoh, that you are in a very different part of India from the fact that all the shopkeepers are women. Some may be Nepali or Cachari, but most are Khasis. Our first view of them was disappointing. All had red mouths from too much *paan* and *koi*, which is the raw form of betel nut and slightly intoxicating. Their teeth, when they smiled, appeared to be worn down to the gums. They were dressed alike in some sort of a shapeless dress or long skirt, and with a piece of check cloth pinned or tied over one shoulder. The checks were small and could be green on white, or blue on white, or red on white. But everyone wore some kind of check in the way I have described. They seemed to be pleasant but shrewd businesswomen. You could bargain with them and enjoy the experience because of the ready smile they produced and their air of good humor, but you would be a very lucky person if you succeeded in bringing the price down.

I could have spent hours in Nongpoh, but the taxi driver was keen to get on, and Frances, too, was feeling a bit unwell. So we had an omelette each, and some fruit, and pushed on. The drive continued much as before, but about ten miles short of Shillong we were suddenly presented with a vision for which no one had prepared us. As the road crested a small hill, we looked down, and there, stretched out for miles before us, was a sheet of grey, green and blue water. The lake, made by damming a river, is appropriately called Barapani. But the Khasis have an even more appropriate name for the river that has been dammed: Umiam, or the river of sorrow. For at certain times it is given to flash floods, and many a young man fishing in it has been carried away in its turbulent water, to be fished out a week later from the lake by sorrowful relatives.

The drive along Barapani is the highlight of the journey. As the road wound, we got views from different angles of the shimmering surface of the lake, now fully exposed, now glimpsed between the branches of trees. And suddenly we realized that those trees weren't the ones we had seen from Gauhati until now, but that we were driving through pine forests.

The Khasi pine—yes, that's the technical term; the Latin is *pinus Khasiana*—is the Cinderella of pines that has not found a good fairy who will redeem her. In comparison to the pine trees of north Indian hill stations it seems stunted. It does not tap well, yielding only small quantities of resin. Nor does it make good furniture. Its distinction is that its needles point upwards. This fact does not make it more attractive, though it might make it a botanical curiosity. I suppose the great thing about the Khasi pine is that it just is, and however inferior it may be as pine, at least it is pine. The Khasis love it.

We were still contemplating pines when we were in Shillong. The entry into Shillong from Gauhati is anticlimactic. I remember a late evening a couple of years later. We were driving up to Kohima in Nagaland from the railhead in Dimapur. We turned a corner, and there, in front of us, was a whole ridge dotted with electric lights, while low over it hung, as out of nothing and in a very dramatic fashion, the full moon. People who go to Kohima always talk about their first view of the city. Shillong can appear spectacular too if you approach it from the south, from Jowai or Cherrapunji. But for the traveler who has chosen to come via Gauhati, Shillong presents a sullen appearance—or non appearance. You pass a petrol pump, then there are a few nondescript houses, then a few more shacks and houses, and then you are there in the very heart of Bara Bazar. It can be disappointing.

We had had a room booked for us in the Legislative Assembly Hostel and got there in pouring rain. Rain, in fact, is the chief of my memories of our early days in Shillong. We announced ourselves to the caretaker and were shown into a large-ish room, rather dark and very damp. We unloaded our belongings from the taxi, paid off the driver, and shut the door. So here we were at last. Our experiences along the way had left us rather tentative and confused about everything. Frances was very tired, and we did not know what he future would bring. But at least we had arrived in Shillong.

The first thing to do was to unpack Cat. He had awakened some hours ago from his drugged sleep, but finding the world just a bit too full of movement right then, had wisely decided to keep his thoughts to himself for the time being. But now, as soon as he was released from two and a half days of drugged imprisonment, he bounded out and, before we could stop him, jumped out of the window. I followed after him, using the somewhat more dignified, if roundabout, method of going through the door and down two corridors into the lawn outside. No Cat.

Frances felt heartbroken. "We didn't bring Cat all the way from Delhi just to lose him as soon as we had arrived here!" she kept saying. She refused dinner and went to bed in tears. There wasn't much I could do to console her, and the truth is that I felt pretty miserable myself. So I, too, got in between the damp sheets, and, so tired was I, fell off to sleep immediately.

About three hours later I was awakened by a peculiar sensation. Something was trying to burrow itself beneath my chin and into the blankets. I opened my eyes, only to find two dimly-seen green things that looked like eyes glittering in the dark. What strange creature could this be? Horrified, I leapt out and turned on the light. There was Cat. He had explored the neighborhood, found it a bit wet outside, and come home through the open window. Unused to the cold, he had decided upon a course of action he had thought rather silly in Delhi, and was now trying to crawl into bed with me.

With Cat back, I knew that Shillong would be an acceptable home for us.

Chapter 2
LIVING THERE

THE NEXT MORNING FRANCES WAS FEELING distinctly unwell and looking quite yellow. Worried, I contacted a university official who found a doctor who said that she was coming down with jaundice, the result, I think, of too many farewell parties in Delhi prior to our departure. This was an emergency for which we had not prepared. The doctor recommended rest and a special diet. Rest she could have in plenty in our room, but peace of mind was going to be difficult when we were living out of suitcases, and the Assembly Hostel kitchen staff frankly confessed their inability to provide a special diet. After some thought I decided that only one thing was possible. She would be more comfortable and get better attention in a hospital room. Once more I consulted the university official and was told to take her to what is still quaintly called the European ward of the Welsh Presbyterian hospital.

The room they gave her was lovely, paneled in dark wood, with an ancient pot-bellied stove and a splendid view of the lawn and beds of giant dahlias. This at least was reassuring: she would not have to put up with the gloomy dampness of the Assembly Hostel.

That left Cat and me in the Hostel. There was a sign inside the wardrobe that said that pets were not allowed, but since Cat was usually out when a man came to clean the room in the morning the officials never found out about him, or if they did, decided that it wasn't worth bothering. Soon I settled into a routine. After an early breakfast I would go off to work. Returning at around 1 p.m. I would give Monster his lunch, read a bit, and then go off to the hospital to see Frances. I'd sit and talk to her till it was time for visitors to leave, and then come back to my room. Cat would be waiting for me to tell him how Frances was. Fortunately, I had progress to report every day. Cat was sympathetic, and encouraged me from time to time by meowing softly. I could see that he was as anxious to have Frances back as soon as possible as I was.

Food presented a problem. At some time in the hoary past the Assembly Hostel kitchen seems to have cooked rather a lot of *dal* and curried chicken bones. Faced, no doubt, with the problem of surplus disposal, they had obviously decided to feed their guests nothing else while stocks lasted. So I had *dal*, chicken bones and rice for breakfast, lunch and dinner. I submitted to this fare for a day and a half, then revolted. Cat didn't mind the bones, though they couldn't have been good for him, but I decided to foray into Police Bazar, which was just a two-minute walk away, to see what could be discovered. What I discovered was R.B. Stores which sold chicken patties. I gratefully devoured four or five of them for dinner, and then went back the next morning for more for breakfast, and then again for lunch. But when dinner time came round again, I thought of the patties and felt sick, and thought of chicken bones and felt sick.

It was in this sickened state that I went to see Frances that evening. The doctors had decided that she was well enough now to have full meals, though her stomach thought otherwise. That is why, as I was sitting talking to her, a nurse brought in steaming soup, fish with white sauce, and a lovely looking pudding. Frances made a groaning sound and pushed the tray away, saying she couldn't bear to look at food. In the meantime, I found I was doing nothing else, and so asked her if it would be all right for me to eat her dinner if she didn't want any. I don't remember now whether I waited for her reply before tucking in; I only remember that for the first time in several days I had a truly satisfactory meal.

Henceforth it became my custom to put up with chicken bones for breakfast, but lunch and dine off hospital food. The nurses assumed, from the way Frances's meals were eaten meticulously down to the last pea, that she was much better already, and doubled her rations. This was just as well, for Frances *was* better and began to want some food herself. By the time she was discharged from the hospital, the nurses were convinced that she had an unusual appetite, for she ate twice as much as a normal human being.

With her discharge a cloud of depression that had settled about me lifted. The day she was leaving the hospital I was informed that a room in the university guest house had fallen vacant, and we could move in there if I chose. I chose.

The guest house, called Dulcie Lodge, was much brighter, more comfortable, and more companionable. Cat found friends of his own species in the neighborhood and was happier too. The only drawback was that after our first night the place became a bit cramped. What happened was this. The room that we moved into had been occupied by a professor who had arrived in Shillong a couple of weeks before us. Being a determined man and not wishing to waste time, he had at once launched a massive house-hunting expedition, and his efforts had soon been rewarded. Thereupon he informed the caretaker that he was vacating his room in the guest house—thus enabling us to move into it— told his wife and son the address of the house he had found, and went off to teach his classes. His family, in the meanwhile, packed their belongings, called a taxi, and went off to occupy the house that their lord and master had found for them. They did not like what they saw. They put up with various inconveniences for a day and a night, but when they found that there wasn't even enough water to brush their teeth, they revolted. The professor's wife informed her husband that she was going back to the guest house, and that henceforth it was she who was going to do the house hunting, not he.

The return of the family posed some problems for us. They insisted on having their old room back; I answered that it had been allotted to us, and that in any case Frances was still convalescing and it would be most inconvenient to move out. Finally, a compromise was worked out. Their bags were deposited in our room, and at night the guest house's parlor served as their bedroom. Everyone was happy.

It was obvious, however, that we would soon have to find housing. Never having rented a house before, I didn't know how or where to begin. Frances suggested advertising in the Sunday paper. This was an excellent idea, except that Shillong had no Sunday papers. I asked my co-lodger for advice, and he said that whenever he met a local man he mentioned his need in the hope that the interlocutor would be able to pull a house out of his hat. My friend's method seemed over-optimistic; but since no other was in sight, I decided to give it a try.

Accordingly, I sought a convenient moment to mention the problem to the first Shillong citizen to whom I was introduced. "You want a house? It's not so easy, my friend." He then gave us his reasons for this pessimistic assessment.

One of the things the Vice Chancellor had told us in Delhi was that housing in Shillong was plentiful and cheap. The reason, he said, was that with the carving out of Meghalaya from Assam, the Assam capital had been shifted from Shillong to a suburb of Gauhati called Dispur, and this had led to a large-scale exodus of Assamese bureaucrats, businessmen, and their families. I got the impression from him that landlords would beg us to occupy their houses, one more desirable than the next.

This, my informant informed me, was not the case. The shifting of the capital had not made much difference, for though the bureaucrats had left, their families were still in Shillong, waiting for their children to finish their schooling. Moreover, what with the creation of the university, the opening of more banks, and the shifting of several all-India institutions and organizations to Shillong, there were, as a matter of fact, far fewer houses available than previously.

This summing up proved to be correct. Indeed, in the last two or three years the situation has got much worse, and it is now almost impossible to find a vacant house in the city that is even half-way decent, and if you are lucky enough to find it, you will have to pay through your nose for it. But at the time of which I am speaking the condition was not so desperate, and I was hopeful that we would find something if only we made a point of letting everybody know of our needs.

We did so, and the results were amazing. Every day some acquaintance or the other mentioned one or two possibilities. Frances was still not strong enough to investigate them with me, so I went on this errand alone. I soon found that though houses existed in Shillong, none of them met with my approval. They were usually damp and tiny little rooms, with corridors that criss-crossed as if designed to resemble a rabbit warren. Several had no sanitary facilities, and a few had no running water. I saw several, and said no every time.

And then a miracle occurred. I was standing one afternoon in the verandah of the guest house sucking disconsolately at my pipe when a jeep drove up and an elderly looking gentleman climbed out with some difficulty and limped up the steps with the help of a cane. He was wearing a jacket, khaki shorts, *puttees*, ankle boots, and a sola topi. A chain from the lower button of his jacket to his pocket indicated that a watch was ticking away in the hidden recesses. When he saw me he asked, in an impeccable accent, if he had the honor of addressing Dr. Singh. I was taken aback. All I could reply was that it wasn't much of an honor, but that yes, I was that person. On hearing that, he took his topi off with a flourish, bowed, and presented me with a note from his pocket.

The note, from a university official, was brief and to the point. It informed me that the bearer was Mr. C. S. Booth, M.B.E., M.C., IAS (Retd.), a former Deputy Commissioner of the Khasi Hills, and that he had a house to rent that might interest us. Impressed,

I invited Mr Booth inside to meet Frances and talk things over over a cup of tea.

The interview was unforgettable. He did not want to rent his house to a pair of strangers without first ascertaining that they were reliable, and to that purpose he began to question us. His very first question shattered me completely.

"Sir," he asked, "did you know Jawaharlal Nehru?"

"No, Sir," I stammered. His disappointment must have been visible, for I tried to make amends by adding, "I am much too young to have known him."

At this he brightened.

"Ah, in that case you must know his daughter Indira."

Well! I could have lied, but such lies are always found out sooner or later. I had to confess that though I knew about the lady in question, I would not assume to call her my friend.

Mr. Booth was disappointed. He obviously liked us and wanted us to have his house. But how could he possibly rent it to us unless we came up to scratch? So far I had got a zero on the exam. He tried to make his next question easier.

"Do you, by any chance, know Chrystal Rogers?"

Some of my readers may know of her. She runs a shelter for stray dogs and cats in Delhi. We had once or twice consulted the vet there regarding Cat. Since I was determined by now to score some marks on this quiz, I replied that though I had never met Ms.

Rogers, we had taken our cat down to her shelter a few times.

"Oh," said Mr. Booth. "You have a cat? I should like to see him."

Fortunately for us, Cat was at home. He was produced with pride, and for once he behaved well in front of a stranger.

"Mister," said Mr. Booth. When he talks to anyone, he calls him or her Mister. "Mister, you look after your cat well."

I thanked him profusely. We had managed to save at least some of our *amour propre*, and faced the next set of questions with some confidence. They were not long in coming.

"Mister," asked Mr. Booth, "do you hunt?"

"No, Sir," I confessed meekly.

"Do you fish?"

"No, Sir," I said, more meekly still.

"Do you collect exotic orchids?"

"No, Sir," I repeated, barely audibly.

"Then, Sir," demanded Mr. Booth, "what do you do?"

Really, this was too much! I summoned what dignity I could and replied, "I teach English."

"Sir," said Mr. Booth witheringly, "any fool can do that. What I mean is, do you have any outdoor interests?"

It so happens that at various times of my life I have collected insects that are found only at high altitudes.

My interest has taken me to Lahaul and Spiti in the Himalayas, the High Atlas mountains in Morocco, and the Sierra Nevada in Spain. My collections are to be found in the School of Entomology, St John's College, Agra, and the Natural History section of the British Museum. So, when I heard Mr. Booth's question, I drew myself up to my full length and said, "Sir, I am a high altitude entomologist."

"Good!" exclaimed Mr. Booth. He had decided that we would be suitable tenants, and was quizzing us only to find out whether we were worthy of the particular house he had in mind. "I think you will like the house. And now, Mister," turning to Frances, "if you have finished your tea, I shall give myself the pleasure of taking both of you in my jeep to see the house I have for you."

Frances said later that she never knew till then that insects had value.

The drive was long and uphill. Finally, when we had left the city behind, we rounded a corner and there were two houses standing in a vast compound full of trees. The bigger one was red and white; the smaller was a cute little doll's house of a cottage with a climber rose round the porch.

"Mister," said Mr. Booth with pride, "you can have both of them."

We looked round. The garden was a pathetic cluster of cosmos and marigolds but afforded possibilities for better things. The bigger house was two stories high, with four wooden-floored and paneled rooms upstairs and two large rooms and a kitchen downstairs. There were two cherry trees on the property, four plum trees, a jacaranda or two, and any number of pine trees. At the back of the house the ground sloped sharply down to a small but pretty waterfall which then flowed on as a stream. Across from this was a pine forest. The university was a ten-minute walk away, the nearest shopping area could be reached in a quarter of an hour. Up here the air was pure and it was very, very quiet. Oddest thing of all, there was a flagpole, left behind by the Central Reserve Police who had occupied the house till recently.

Mr. Booth pointed out some other desirable features. As is customary in hill stations, the house came furnished. The doll's house could be used as a guest house for friends who visited us during the fishing season. There would also doubtless be other friends who preferred to sleep under canvas; for them, said Mr. Booth, there was an open space where they could pitch their tents. In the garage was a hammock for use in the garden during the summer, and a *machan* which we could take along with us when we went to watch rhino and wild elephants in the forests of Assam.

We were charmed. I did not imagine that we would be using the *machan* much—we never did, in fact—or that fishermen friends (we did not have any) would come and camp outside, but the idea of having Mr.

Booth as our landlord was irresistible. Besides, we argued, there wasn't much point in living in a hill station unless one could live on a hill instead of down in the flat bazar area, which most people preferred. Ours was one of the higher hills of Shillong, and there was something to be said, too, for looking down on the others from here. But could we afford the place? Mr. Booth must have guessed our thoughts, for he said that whereas the assessed rent was Rs. 503, he would be willing to let us have it for Rs. 450. It happened that that was our maximum limit, and so a deal was struck.

The house required a few improvements and repairs. Mr. Booth promised to have them done in ten days' time, and thereupon we fixed a date, about two weeks distant, when we would move in. That date happened to be our first wedding anniversary.

We were elated at our find, but when we told friends about it they looked glum. No one would tell us what their specific reservations were, but one and all gave us to understand, by their looks and tone of voice, that we had not made a wise decision. Finally, the wife of a colleague, less reticent than the others, spilled the beans.

"Frances," she told my wife, "the house is haunted."

Neither Frances nor I are superstitious, and we pooh-poohed the suggestion. But our friend was adamant.

"When you next go to the house," she said, "see if there isn't a red cross on top of the roof. If there is, you mark my words, the house is haunted. I have many Khasi friends, and they all tell me that a red cross on a rooftop is a sure sign that there is something evil about the house."

Well, you can be sure that the next day I went and looked. There was a perfectly ordinary lightning conductor, painted red in keeping with the color of the roof, but there wasn't anything extraordinary about it as far as I could see. But our friend was not convinced. She just kept shaking her head and saying, "You mark my words!"

Frances was impervious to this, but I decided to consult a few more people. When I asked them bluntly whether the house was supposed to be haunted, they looked uncomfortable and finally muttered something about not being superstitious themselves, but they had heard from someone—of course, such stories were not to be believed, but, etc., etc. …At first, I laughed the whole thing off.

"The ghost will run away when he sees us," I said. Or, "We'll drop iron plates on his toes and make him limp the rest of his life. Or, better still, we'll hide all the red ink away from him, and then he won't be able to go around making blood stains on the floor." I remained flippant even when it was pointed out that there was a graveyard not far from the house. But when a perfectly sober and presumably honest businessman who had lived in Shillong for twenty years said that he knew of a murder that had been committed in the house,

I began to wonder myself. I shared my doubts with Frances, only to be snubbed immediately.

By now Mr. Booth had nearly completed the repairs that were to precede our move into the house, and I reflected wryly that even if it were haunted, there was precious little I could do about it at this late stage. We'll just have to take the house now, come ghost or high water, I said to myself.

Later we discovered why the house was regarded as haunted. It belonged to Mr. Booth. In Hindi, and presumably in Khasi, that would be "the house of Booth." But Booth sounds like *bhoot*, the Hindi (and probably Khasi) word for ghost. So the house came to be known as "*bhoot ghar*" or haunted house.

The day arrived when we had to move in, and of course it had to pour. We were just wondering what we would do when Mr. Booth arrived with jeep, trailer, tarpaulin, and four porters. "Mister, I've come to help you move," was all he said to us. Then he broke into rapid-fire Khasi, instructing the porters to lift our crates carefully, carry the fridge upright, and make sure that everything was properly secured and covered in the trailer. Three trips he and his men made in pouring rain between the guest house, situated at one end of Shillong, and our new house at the other, and in the third trip Frances and I were accommodated too.

But not Cat. For, in his usual perverse way, Cat had gone out very early in the morning, and when it was time for us to move, could be found nowhere. So we left instructions with the guest house staff, who had got to know him quite well by now, that when he returned he was to be secured and not allowed to run away, and that we would return the following day to take him with us.

When we reached the house in pouring rain, we were amazed at what we saw. Under the supervision of Mr. Booth's son, his men had stacked our crates very neatly into the house, a carpenter was standing ready with hammer and chisel to unpack them as we desired, our bedding had been undone and our beds were already made. And even as we stood admiring all this, hot cups of tea appeared as if by magic. Mr. Booth is an absolute marvel!

He helped us unpack a few things and establish some order. By now it was evening, and we were just about ready for an early night in bed. When he saw the condition we were in, he said he would leave us. We came with him to his jeep to see him off and thank him. And then, just before he got in, he did something that was as touching as it was unexpected. He took off his sola topi, bowed, and said: "Mister, now I take my leave. I wish you a very good night, and a very happy stay in my house." With that, he was gone.

We slept soundly, undisturbed by any ghosts. I woke up the next morning to brilliant sunshine, went to the bathroom, turned on the tap, and found that there wasn't a drop of water. I was standing there not knowing what to do when I heard a jeep drive up, and Mr. Booth appeared at the door.

"Mister, did you sleep well?" he inquired.

I said I had, but this morning we were facing the problem of having no water.

A look of great consternation passed over his face.

"Mister, just wait a bit. I'll be back soon." And with that he hobbled back to his jeep.

A quarter of an hour later he drove up again, looking triumphant. Attached to the back of his jeep was his trailer, and resting solidly in it was a twenty-gallon drum full of water.

Later in the day he made another trip, this time with Cat. Cat had returned to the guest house the night after we had left at his usual time of 2 a.m. Not knowing that we weren't there, he had jumped straight into the bed I usually occupied. But, that night, it was occupied by another guest who was rudely awakened from his slumbers by an unknown creature, invisible in the dark, clawing his forehead with his paws. He shrieked and shot out of bed; but when the staff, who rushed in at the noise, found that it was only a rather bewildered-looking cat who couldn't understand what all this fuss was about, they captured him and shut him in his basket, where Mr. Booth found him the next day, and in which he transported him to us.

A prince among men. That's what Mr. Booth is.

We settled down quickly Mr. Booth was our frequent and most welcome visitor, and when we heard his jeep we would rush out to greet him. He is a man of rare experience and many talents. He often talked about his life, and we were glad to listen. One of his English ancestors had fought in the Mutiny, and one of his grandmothers was a Prussian lady. Judging from the photograph that hangs in his living room, she must have been a strict woman with a high sense of duty. Mr. Booth started life as a tea planter but joined the Assam Civil Service shortly afterwards. During the Second War he was a captain in the Pioneers and saw service in Burma. He developed a limp when his jeep went over a mine. He was decorated for his services during the War, and joined the IAS after independence. He was Deputy Commissioner of the Khasi Hills for six years, which is a record for these parts. As a young man he walked all over the north-east, in Assam, Manipur, and Nagaland; and wherever he went, he took his gun, his rod and his dogs. He speaks any number of tribal languages, and knows the ways of all who inhabit the tribal areas of north-east India, animals as well as men. Since he was widowed, he has spent a good deal of time on a small farm just outside Gauhati. He has known many men, ranging from British governors to Naga headhunters, and often regaled us with anecdotes connected with them: how Rivett-Carnac built a certain house, or "Aching" Payne used to go out fishing in a certain stream, or how Sir Keith Cantlie became so old that he had to walk with a hoop. From him we learnt a great deal, not only about

Shillong but about the whole of the tribal belt of the north-east. It was he who first made us interested in the people of this region and gave us a sense of history and perspective in thinking about them.

Mr. Booth wanted us to give our house a name, and this occasioned many discussions between Frances and myself. She suggested Edgewood and Edgehill as being appropriate descriptions of the setting and location of the house. Mr. Booth vetoed both. "Mister, Bing Cholmondolay called his house Edgehill, and soon after drank himself to death in '04. And Mrs. Holder's house, now occupied by a Marwari gentleman, is still called Edgewood." I, rather facetiously, suggested Touchwood. Too flippant, said Frances. Finally we both hit upon the same name at once: Arden. It was Shakespearean and therefore befitted our profession. It suggested a beautiful idyll, of which the house held possibilities. And had we not come to Shillong to find tongues in trees, books in the running brooks, sermons in stones, and good in everything?

"I would not change it," Mr. Booth capped the quotation delightedly. Really, it is amazing how much he knows. He even quotes Shakespeare.

So our house became Arden, and Mr. Booth had a board painted and nailed picturesquely to a pine tree at the gate. We felt quite pleased too, till John Roche came to spend a week with us as our first guest. John and I were at Oxford together. He now teaches English in Sydney, and was on his way to England for a sabbatical. He took one of the best Firsts in my year, and knows his Shakespeare backwards.

He got out of the taxi and saw the board. He was very tired, not having slept since he took off from Sydney what seemed like years ago. But Shakespeare overcomes all such obstacles. His eyes twinkling, he quoted: "Now I am in Arden; the more fool I; when I was at home I was in a better place." And then, feeling perhaps that he was being rude to his hosts, he mended matters by clapping me on the back and saying: "But travelers must be content!"

Curiosity prompted us to compare our house with others'. We were surprised to find that although stone is quarried in and around Shillong, it was not used for building houses, until Mr. Booth told us why. Shillong was established by the British in 1875, and all the earliest houses were indeed of stone. But they were all destroyed, and several people killed, in the earthquake of 1895. Thereafter all houses have been built in what is called the Assam style. Government House, now Raj Bhawan, the oldest building in Shillong, was the first to use this style; the Chief Secretary's bungalow, the second oldest building, followed suit. Apparently even architecture bows before hierarchy. Since then, this style has become ubiquitous. It is true that the houses of several Marwari businessmen look as though they were lifted straight out of Jodhpur, and some rich builders, with more money than sense, have gone in for the reinforced cement and concrete type of construction that you find all over the plains. But the former style looks incongruous in Shillong, and the latter, apart from polluting the landscape, has a more practical drawback. Cement and concrete houses are cold and damp in a city where one's major endeavor for a good part of the year is to keep cold and damp out. I know one colleague who lived in such a house. He ran up astronomical electric bills by keeping electric heaters going all through the year, and every day his wife had to daub the floors with a piece of rag to get rid of all the moisture.

So the Assam style, for all its drawbacks, has established itself as the dominant architectural style all through the city. It means that houses are built on stilts, or, as ours was, upon a small cement plinth which rises off the ground by about a foot. The floors are wooden, and the roofs of tin or corrugated iron. Quite often they are painted red, though black paint, being much cheaper, is also used. The walls are made of bamboo rushes, which are then plastered on the inside as well as the outside. The whole outside of the house is usually encased in tin sheeting, and sometimes the inner walls are paneled with wood. The tin sheeting is put in such a way that a bit of space is left between it and the bamboo-and-mud wall. This space acts as an excellent insulator and keeps the house warm and dry. But it also provides rats with a marvelous space for nesting, and there are few houses in Shillong that do not have rats. Ours didn't, thanks to Cat. Not that he went after them; indeed, if a mouse ever scurried from under his nose, he would sniff and turn his head the other way in disgust. But the rats obviously didn't like his feline smell, so I suppose it could be said that he odorized them away.

These houses are pretty and comfortable, but they do require a lot of maintenance. If the walls are not repaired, and rotten bamboos replaced, the house will be a wreck within a very few years. This has given rise to a large class of *mistries* or carpenters and general handymen whose services are among the more essential ones in Shillong. They are versatile, and can do everything from fixing a leaking tap to building a whole house. And they are among the best makers of fireplaces and chimneys in India. A fireplace is a must in most homes in Shillong because of the weather, and all through the winter a characteristic smell in the evenings is that of the acrid smoke which is produced from burning Jowai coal, a variety high in sulphur content, and therefore not favored by industry, but one which burns brightly and with plenty of heat in domestic hearths and is mined in the neighboring Jowai hills. A great deal of skill goes into the making of a satisfactory fireplace. One that is too big and deep may be all right for log fires, but for coal fires a smaller, narrower one is required. It must be placed in a corner of the room, not in the center of any wall, and to decide which corner will radiate heat best requires nice judgement. The best stone for backing is sillimanite, which is quarried in few places outside Meghalaya, and whose great quality is that it is highly heat resistant. Once upon a time it was used for the manufacture of spark plugs and all kinds of other things, and a private quarrying firm made a lot of money out of it. The firm even had its own private aeroplane—the height of luxury in India. But then substitutes for sillimanite were developed, and now it is used for little more than fireplaces, though a government agency has come forward to quarry the stone in place of the private firm.

Finally, the angle at which the backing of the fireplace is placed is of the utmost importance. If it is too acute, smoke will fill the room instead of going up the chimney; if it is not acute enough, as happens sometimes in houses whose builders have not employed the local *mistries*, the heat will escape up the chimney with the smoke.

The Khasi are, as a rule, very house proud, and you will hardly ever find a Khasi house which is not thoroughly clean and tidy. The Khasi are, in fact, a very clean people. One of their favorite pastimes is washing—the washing of clothes, the washing of dishes, the washing of their own persons. Every Sunday each Khasi family does its week's laundry, which, apart from performing an important hygienic function, also provides a social occasion for the women to gather at the wash tap to exchange gossip. After they have done their laundry, they turn their attention to themselves, and while bathing rub, rub, rub their feet with a flat, abrasive stone till their feet are absolutely pink. Few Khasis feel happy unless they have a liberal supply of this stone handy, and I know of at least one Khasi lady who was absolutely miserable in Delhi till her relatives in Shillong sent her two of these stones by parcel post.

Another item for cleaning that the Khasi like to have in abundance is the broom. I know from experience that Khasi brooms are infinitely better made than those that you get in Delhi. They are made from a special kind of plant, of which several households grow at least one in their gardens. The Khasi broom reaches into the most hidden recesses and corners, and is a sworn enemy of dirt. And then, after the house has been swept, the average Khasi wife will polish the floor as lovingly as she will tend her baby. The usual method is to use a mixture of candle wax and kerosine, with a touch of a kind of soap called *ptheng*. This last-named ingredient ensures that the polished floor will not be sullied by footmarks. You spread a little bit of this concoction on the floor, and then you rub it into the wooden floor with a rough gunny sack till the wood glows. The harder and longer the rubbing, the greater the shine; and some Khasis regard the rubbing and polishing of floors as their favorite hobby. When they have a spare half hour, they will go down on their hands and knees and rub and rub and rub. It is, perhaps, revealing that when the North-Eastern Hill University (NEHU) advertised for three women cleaners in the Class

IV category of employment, they received over two hundred applications. Interviews were held, and the only question asked of each candidate was how many kinds of floor polish she had had the experience of using. The jobs went to the candidates with the widest experience, but even those who were not selected had used Mansion polish, which is pretty expensive, at some stage.

If this kind of attention to polish makes the average Khasi home a pleasure to visit, wait till you go into the kitchen. I never knew that metal vessels and dishes could be made to sparkle so. The secret this time is steel wool. Steel wool is used in the plains too, but not as widely or skillfully as in the Khasi hills. Besides, not every kind of steel wool will do. A Khasi girl on her first visit to Delhi as a domestic help asked her employers to get her some steel wool. The employers went all round the city and finally managed to find a bundle in, I think, Safdarjang. But their help was not satisfied. The only good steel wool, according to her, was Ganesh brand, whereas the employers had brought her Big Rat brand.

Clearly, we would have to work very hard indeed if we were to win the Khasis' approval for the way we kept our house, and not be branded by them as dirty people from the plains.

In our attempts to do our house up we were helped and encouraged, as always, by Mr. Booth. He introduced us to such mysteries as the staining and polishing of floors, lighting fires, and learning to tell good Jowai coal from inferior. More important, he furnished the house for us. Rental houses in Shillong come furnished, though the amount and quality of the furniture varies from landlord to landlord. You can be sure of finding two beds, usually two Khasi beds, made of unseasoned pine and not much more than five and a half feet in length, so that sleeping in them can be a somewhat Procrustean experience; also, a couple of tables and chairs. Sometimes you may be lucky and get a wardrobe thrown in for good measure, otherwise you will find yourself having to buy one sooner or later, since the walls of Assam type houses make built-in wardrobes impossible. But we were probably the only tenants to be given also two massive, and for us necessary, bookshelves. Mr. Booth also gave us a bench that looked as though it must have put in time in some dentist's waiting room. "Mister," he explained, "this is where your students can sit in the verandah while they are waiting to see you."

We had a hard time convincing him that if students came, they would be welcomed in our living room rather than be asked to wait outside. Finally, he understood, and took the bench away, but thought that the absence of the bench should be made up in some other manner. Frances unwittingly gave him an opportunity. She said one day, apropos of nothing, and without thinking of the consequences, that she had always fancied an oval dining table. The next day we came home to find that the rectangular dining table which Mr. Booth had given us had disappeared, and in its place was a beautiful oval one! On another occasion he brought, without any provocation at all, a really magnificent roll-top desk. "Mister," he told Frances, "a lady like you should write her letters only at a desk like this."

Once Mr. Booth starts, there is no stopping him. As I mentioned earlier, the kitchen was downstairs; and since it was large, it served us as the dining room as well. But he probably thought that it was lowering the dignity of his house for his tenants to eat in the kitchen. In any case, he did not approve of Frances running up and down the stairs all day, though he was inclined to believe that it would do my figure no harm. So he took matters in hand. One day we found some *mistries* digging trenches right next to the house, and when we remonstrated they said they were acting on Mr. Booth's orders, which were that the foundation should be dug forthwith for a new kitchen. We protested as strongly to Mr. Booth as we could, since it was going too far to build a whole new kitchen for us, but to no avail. He made only one concession: he could not, he said, make it too big, but Frances could design it just as she pleased. The final product turned out to be about fifteen feet by twelve, with a lot of light, and the sink, shelves, counters and power outlets just where we wanted them. There couldn't have been a nicer kitchen to work in.

With the new kitchen ready, it was time to turn our attention to the garden. Here we suffered from two handicaps. The soil was very poor, being highly acidic and mostly sand, and neither Frances nor I was any good at making plants grow. Mr. Booth remedied the first drawback by binging jeep-loads of good earth and filling flower beds with it, but even he could not remedy the second. He was joined, in his attempts, by all our neighbors who wanted us to have at least some semblance of a garden. They would bring us, from time to time, seeds, or seedlings, or cuttings of plants they thought would do well and didn't require much attention. When a neighbor who was from Mizoram found that we were intrigued by a vegetable he was growing, he brought some young plants along and insisted on planting them in our vegetable patch himself because, he said, it was a Mizo vegetable and required the special touch of a Mizo to grow well. From then on he would drop in of an evening, inquire after the garden, and tell us whether a particular plant was getting too little water or too much shade, or whether it was time to start preparing beds for a particular flower.

The tribals of the north-east, we discovered, love gardens and are naturally very talented at making things grow. Every house, no matter how poor, has a small patch of ground for a few flowers and vegetables. The annual flower show is, next to church going, the most popular draw, and so many people come to look at the exhibits, judge them critically, and also judge the judgements of the judges who have awarded the prizes, that you have barely room to stand. They are aided, in the cultivation of their hobby, by the weather of Shillong. Everything will grow there. Our friend Gen. Kulkarni, who was one of the finest gardeners in Shillong, used to say that if a flower could grow anywhere in the world, it would thrive in Shillong. Certainly we ourselves had cherries growing next to bananas, and I don't know of any other place in the world where the temperate and the sub-tropical coexist so harmoniously Whether it is the common marigold, the tough daisy, the decorative verbena, the beautiful pansy, the lovely phlox, the delicate and exotic gloxinia, or the rare lady's slipper orchid, they can be, and are, all found even in the ordinary gardens of Shillong, such as ours definitely was.

Thanks to the help of various people, we were able to have a fairly reasonable garden in two years. It was certainly not one of the glories of Shillong, but gave us much pleasure. Frances especially plunged literally up to her elbows in the work. Whenever she had time, she would be digging, or weeding, or sweeping, or watering, or transplanting, or doing one of those numerous chores that may be back-breaking work, but are the gardener's delight. But the garden was too big for her alone, and I regret to say that I didn't prove to be a terribly enthusiastic worker. So we hired a gardener. Nageshwar is a very fine young man, polite, charming, and eager to please. He is also known to have been at work in the garden on occasion. But his major interest in life was how to get a permanent Class IV post in the central government, and so his presence didn't lighten Frances's tasks materially. Not that she minded. Indeed, in the course of time she became quite adept at producing rather fine beds of astors, pansies, carnations, and the biggest marigolds you have ever seen. I am pretty certain that her marigolds would have won at least a consolation prize at the flower show. But we never exhibited, and were none the less happy for that. In the meanwhile, I learnt to specialize in french beans, which we harvested in great abundance during the monsoon months; and when the crop was finished, used the same beds for sweet peas. The first year we planted them we produced exactly two flowers, but we got better as we went on, and the supreme moment came when both Mr. Booth and our Mizo neighbor complimented us on them and asked for their seeds.

Our greatest success was not, however, of our doing but Nature's. There was a squash creeper in the vegetable patch, and come the monsoon it would be absolutely laden with the vegetable. We ate as much as we could, and took huge baskets to friends But sometimes we would be embarrassed by meeting our friends on the road carrying huge baskets of squash to dump on us.

The Khasi squash is unlike any that you can get in the plains. Tastier, it is also smaller, club shaped, and prickly. The Khasi word for it, we discovered, is *piskot*. The locals cook it in an astonishing variety of ways. They boil it, fry it, curry it with meat or all by itself, and sometimes eat it raw. They also salt it, pickle it, dry it, bake it, and sometimes bury it, digging it out months later when it is yellow and shriveled, to season their food with. Every three years or so they dig out the root and eat that. A truly versatile vegetable indeed.

The business of exchanging seeds and seedlings is, I found, common in Shillong and provides an excellent topic for conversation and a way of getting to know people. There were many families whose names we did not know, but to whom we referred as the yellow rose people, or the dahlia tree family. If we liked a flower in someone's garden, we would just march in, introduce ourselves, and request a cutting. We met with only welcome and delight on such occasions. If anyone asked us for a cutting or a plant, we were equally delighted to oblige. This proved an ideal way of breaking the ice between our neighbors and ourselves, and the beginning of several friendships. We discovered that the flowers that people valued most, and which can be referred to as the pride of Shillong, were the giant begonia and orchids of all varieties. We were successful with neither.

The giant begonia is grown from bulbs, which even those who are not very well to do will import at considerable cost from Darjeeling. It is a difficult flower to grow but is truly lovely, and looks a little bit like a rose, though without the fragrance. It comes in a great variety of colors and shades. Red is considered common by some, but is perhaps the most attractive. I approve of begonias. The orchids are a different matter. Every garden has at least one bunch, usually tied to a tree or, if a tree is not available, to a piece of wood which is then suspended from the roof of the house. There is, I am told, a large number of species, the rarest being those that come from Mizoram. Orchid collecting is one of the common pastimes in Shillong, and young and not so young people go out with long sticks with a hook at one end into the forests to find rare varieties. The government doesn't approve at all, and at several places stern warnings have been posted warning depredators of the strict consequences that might follow. But I have never known a serious orchid collector to fall foul of the law. These orchids are brought back, lovingly tied to bits of wood and moss, and hung out on trees. But not any tree will do. Some are better hosts than others. The jacaranda, for instance, is preferred to the pine. There the orchid hangs, looking most ordinary and doing nothing for the greater part of the year, while it is watched dotingly by the owners. Then, once a year, and sometimes for very short periods, it flowers

The event is climactic to orchid lovers. I do not rank among them, and always found the flowering a let-down. For one thing I find that the rarer and more prized the orchid, the uglier its flower is likely to be. I once remarked on a rather pretty blue flower, only to be told by my companion that it was the common Blue Wanda. If I wanted to see something really worthwhile, I should visit his garden. I did, and was shown a plant. I couldn't even tell which the leaves were and which the flowers, they looked so alike. "Ah," said my friend, "that is what makes this species so marvelous." I could not help thinking of J-K. Huysmans' hero des Esseintes who valued flowers in proportion as they were ugly and looked artificial.

No, I don't hold by orchids. We had a few, thanks to Mr. Booth, and enjoyed their yellow, black-centered flowers while they lasted. But Mr. Booth had informed us early on that they were quite common; and finding that we could not even remember the Latin names he used to rattle off most impressively, wisely decided that this was an area where it was hopeless even to try and educate us. Therefore, though he gave us many lovely plants for our garden, he gave us no more orchids.

What I enjoyed above all were the flowering trees and shrubs. Azaleas flowered in the early summer, pink and red and white. The jacaranda was a lovely blue. In early December came the cherry blossoms, beautiful though short lived. We had two cherry trees, and one of my great pleasures was seeing them in bloom as I crested a mound every afternoon on my way home from work.

They always reminded me of Housman's poem:

Loveliest of trees, the cherry now
Is hung with bloom along the bough.

It's a slight, sentimental poem, but summed up my feelings.

The cherries invited depredations. Every once in a while, we would find that a passer-by had lopped off a twig, and sometimes a whole branch, with which to decorate his house. Though we minded this damage to the trees, we always had enough blossoms to give us pleasure.

Shortly afterwards would bloom the yellow mimosa, or the Australian wattle. According to Mr. Booth the seed for the tree was imported from Australia early in the century by one Mrs. Holder. She tried planting it, but with no success till her correspondent in Australia told her to boil the seed. Thereafter it grew in such profusion that, as you go up to, and past, upper Shillong, you pass through whole forests of nothing but this tree. There was some talk at one stage of using its bark for tanning leather, but no tanneries were set up, and the tree exists for no other purpose than to delight the beholder with its flowers. It can, however, have a positive use in the future. Belonging as it does to the leguminous family, it is a nitrogen fixer. If, as seems likely, forests are cut down to make land available for agriculture, the Australian wattle will prove to have been more useful in death than it has been so far in life. May that day be truly distant!

Tripping on the heels of the mimosa would come the blossoms of the fruit trees, the plum, the peaches and the pears, and then suddenly the wisteria, the japonica and the yellow jasmine would be in full bloom. One doesn't have to know much about flowers to be interested in them; and if one is interested—as who, living in Shillong, can afford not to be?—there will be enough pleasure for him to offset the irritations that all flesh is heir to.

Another compensation can be pets. We had Cat, of course, who quickly made a home for himself in his new abode. When we first moved into Arden, we also found three dogs on the compound. Frances named them Fawn, Jack and Charity. Fawn and Jack resisted our efforts to make friends and left soon after our arrival. But Charity stayed. She was very odd colored, almost blue, and very, very old. She had had, we were told, at least seven basketfuls of pups, all with that distinctive coloring; and even today, whenever you see a stray dog that has a rather unusual color, you can be almost sure that he has descended from her. Charity loved the food we gave her, she loved going with us for walks, and she loved sneaking into the kitchen, with the result that we had to be sure at all times that all the doors were properly secured. One thing she was not was a watch dog. She loved people, and whoever came, friend or foe, she would wag her tail and proffer her nose to be scratched. She was particularly fond of my head of department, Dr. George, though he was no great lover of Charity. Once, when my wife had started teaching at NEHU, the caretaker of the building an ex-Army corporal named Cherian, knocked at the door of her classroom, entered, saluted her smartly, and said, "Sir," (like Mr. Booth, Cherian knew no distinction based on gender), "Sir, your beautiful Alsatian dog is sitting on Dr. George's desk, and Dr. George is not liking it." Well, Dr. George may not have been amused, but we were at the way Charity, the most mongrel of mongrels, had been promoted to the status of a pedigreed animal. On another occasion Charity followed us to Dr. George's house, but deciding, through a piece of rather perverted logic, that we would leave through the back door took up her station there. However, we left through the front, and not finding Charity there, assumed that she had gone back home, as she often did. Charity, on the other hand, being a loyal dog, decided to wait for us all night long. She had been sneaking much too frequently into our kitchen lately, with the result that her tummy was not quite in order. I don't like to contemplate the scene that must have confronted Dr. George the next morning when he went out through the back door for his morning walk.

As she grew older, Charity grew feebler, and one winter afternoon she was dead. With a heavy heart I buried her as I had previously buried one of her pups. Shortly afterwards I had to bury another of our acquisitions, a dappled white and brown puppy called

Motley. He was bitten by a rabid dog, and though we tried to save him through a course of injections, he died on the seventeenth day.

Our next puppy was brought to us by a neighbor. She was white with black eyes. Frances called her *Kajal*. She was timid, and did not jump and play as puppies at that age should. Our friend Jan Conway (more about her later) was surprised. As she said, he ought to be romping around. So I rechristened her Romper, and then she came out of her shell and began to romp around indeed, much to the detriment of our garden. She soon acquired a boy friend. Lion was the scarred veteran of many a dog fight. Tawny colored, and with gleaming yellow eyes, he could look frightening but was extremely gentle, and greatly devoted to Romper. When we went for walks Romper and Lion would come along too. Romper, one of whose ancestors must have been a hound, would gallop down the path at electric speed, burrow into rabbit holes, and generally galumph quite happily, while Lion trotted sedately by our side, tail up in the air, admiring his girlfriend's talents but showing no desire to emulate them. From time to time, Romper would stop and beckon Lion to join her, whereupon he would trot a bit faster towards her, wagging his tail. Romper would wait till he was almost there, and then, with a bound, be off again, turning her head round from time to time with mockery in her eyes. Then Lion would look us at us sheepishly, and grin. You may not believe it, but it is true: Lion could grin. You said, "Lion, grin!" and a sparkle would come into his eyes and his lips would part to reveal his teeth. This was the only trick he knew, nor did we teach our dogs any others. For one thing, they had no academic ability and wouldn't have learned.

When Romper became pregnant, we were sure that the father was Lion. The puppies were born underneath the house, and for three weeks, though we heard them, we had no means of knowing how many there were or what they looked like. Then, one morning, Romper squeezed herself out and was followed by one, two, three—*eight* puppies, yelping and stumbling and trying to clamber everywhere, and falling down, and starting again. They had enormous appetites, and for a few days our milk bill went up. But they were Romper's pups, and Romper, for some reason, was tremendously popular with our neighbors. In no time all the pups were spoken for. I had a moment of doubt one day when a neighbor said that he'd take two pups when they were old enough to eat crops. I had visions of two energetic young dogs devastating field after field of corn. But what he meant was nothing more than that they should be old enough to eat cereals—which, in the local context, means cooked rice—and the puppies soon established that they could. Thereupon they all found good homes.

When they had first appeared before us, Lion had received a shock For it was obvious that it was not he but another casual canine visitor who was the father. But he put up with this insult to his malehood with good grace; and though he never became over-friendly with the young ones, put up with them peacefully enough. In spite of this treachery on Romper's part his affection for her never wavered, and they may still be seen living happily together in Arden. A friend informs us that Romper is pregnant again; let's hope that this time the joy of fatherhood will really go to Lion.

Romper and Lion, like Charity, are extremely friendly. Lion, indeed, can be jealous of other male dogs who try from time to time to make Romper's acquaintance, but towards human beings, male or female, both are gentleness itself. They never barked at people, and this rather upset me at times. After all, what use is a dog who won't warn his masters of approaching danger? When Romper was young, I assumed that she would learn to bark in due course; but when six months had passed and the only sounds she continued to produce were a whimper saying "please scratch my ears," I decided that the matter was serious and required my attention. So, for about six weeks afterwards, I gave her lessons in barking for an hour every day, Sundays and other holidays not excluded. She would cock her ears and look at me quizzically, trying to make out what I was saying; but the problem was that I barked in English and Hindi, while she, being a Khasi, spoke only that language.

My efforts ended rather abruptly one day when some friends inquired very solicitously of Frances whether I had been working too hard lately, or was under stress or pressure of any sort.

Thereafter I did the only thing possible: I started a propaganda war. I put up a big sign at the gate saying "Beware of Dog," and informed all and sundry that Romper was a real terror who wouldn't allow any strangers near the house. I cannot swear that my methods succeeded, but it remains true that no thieves or robbers ever paid us the courtesy of a nocturnal visit. In the meanwhile, Romper continues, in her illiterate way, to refuse to take the hint that the sign gives.

Or maybe I am wrong after all and Romper is cleverer than I am willing to grant. Maybe she knew she could keep undesirables away, but also that she should not disturb our nocturnal rest. So she invented a particular kind of growl, one that is uttered at such a frequency that it does not disturb the sound sleeper, but is enough to send gentlemen of the night scuttling away in chill terror.

Chapter 3
FRIENDS

$\mathscr{I}$F, BEFORE WE WENT TO SHILLONG, ANYONE HAD asked us from what kind or class of people we expected most of our new friends to be drawn, I suppose we should have answered that they were likely to be academics associated with NEHU. It is quite common to find people whose friends belong to the same professional community as themselves, share the same social and cultural interests, and possess more or less similar expectations and ways of living. This, at any rate, is true of me. Most of my friends are teachers, and my normal expectation would have been that the pattern would continue unbroken in Shillong.

As it turned out, this was not to be. Two of the people in the English department of NEHU, of which I was a member, had, indeed, been friends of mine for years, and we continue friends still. But one of them, Noorul Hasan, left NEHU shortly after I arrived in Shillong to do higher studies abroad, and the other, Prabhu Guptara, followed suit the following year. Thus I was not able to renew and further consolidate old friendships in NEHU. For the rest, the scene that struck me was bleak. Maybe the fault lies in Frances and myself, but we were just not able to care very much for a majority of NEHU's burgeoning faculty. I have often tried to explain to myself why this was so. One is not, after all, obliged to like all the people one works with, but to have liked so few—as I say, the fault was most probably ours. But the NEHU faculty was a peculiar bunch of people too, as several unbiased friends who visited us from Delhi and elsewhere from time to time seemed to think. For one thing, it soon became apparent that some, at least, of my new colleagues were fugitives, trying to run away from their past and perhaps from themselves. They had not got on too well with people in other universities, perhaps, and so had come to Shillong which was far enough away for them to be able to make a new start. Or they were disgruntled in their previous jobs because of a lack of promotion or for other reasons, and so had come to NEHU in the hope that they would be able to go a rung or two up the ladder of success. A few may have had personal or family reasons for wanting to be as far from their previous places of work as possible. Whatever the reasons—and the ones I have suggested are at best conjectural—we found that NEHU faculty was unable to cohere into a community, much less a happy and creative and purposeful family. There was a good deal of suspicion, jealousy and intrigue. Since no one felt secure, working as he or she was in a totally new environment, and with people they didn't know, no one felt really at ease. This sense of insecurity led to cliquishness, or to a kind of guarded watchfulness, or else to an out and out each-man-for-himself attitude. There was much talk but little camaraderie, much discussion about NEHU but little of that relaxed, concerned, intellectual give and take, and high-spirited fun which I have come to associate with friends and friendship. What was particularly disappointing was the way in which a few of the younger teachers almost fresh out of university tended to adopt the attitudes of their seniors. However, many young people were, on the whole, more interesting than the older ones, and we tended to get on far better with them, and enjoyed meeting many of them socially. But to them, I suppose, we were the older generation; and we missed in them the frankness, eagerness, and the easy acceptance of youth. We sensed in some a kind of shiftiness born of a feeling that they were being watched and judged, in others an arrogance that came perhaps from their being considered the Vice Chancellor's blue-eyed boys who were entitled to perks and promotions, and in yet others a timidity as a result of an uncommon awareness of rank and hierarchy.

Indeed, the deep and all-pervasive sense of hierarchy that characterized NEHU proved ultimately to be the greatest single enemy of natural human relationships. Hierarchies are bad everywhere and I detest them; in a university they are pernicious. Yet NEHU ran as an hierarchical system. A Reader was more important than a Lecturer, a Professor more important than a Reader, a Dean more important than a Professor. In the running of the university only heads of departments were consulted. Only they were invited to the social get-togethers that the university sometimes organized in honor of distinguished visitors, People took offense if they weren't addressed as "Doctor" or "Professor" in conversation, or if they received a note from a colleague with the salutation "Dear Ram" (or Shyam, or Tom, or Dick, or whatever) rather than "Dear Professor so-and-so." In introducing themselves, several tended to say "I am Doctor (or Professor) so-and-so, Head of the Department of such-and-such." To laugh at this pomposity was regarded as bad form.

Under such circumstances we decided quite early in our stay at NEHU that it was not from our colleagues that our friends would be drawn. We did ultimately form two or three good friendships with teachers like Mrinal and Sujata Miri or Temsula Ao, but most of our friends came from non-academic circles. Looking back, this was not a bad thing at all. It is wrong to mix too exclusively with one's own kind.

Our first friend in Shillong was, of course, Mr. Booth, and he remained our best friend all the time we were there. Shortly after our arrival, and even before we met Mr. Booth, we got to know the Duaras. A student in Delhi had mentioned, before we left, that his uncle Bapu Duara lived in Shillong, and we could call on him for any help we wanted. Of course almost the first thing we wanted on arrival was a house, and when it was suggested that Mr. Duara might have one to rent, I decided to call on him, both because of his nephew and for the sake of a possible house.

The house never materialized: it had been sold just the day before to a businessman who was thinking of pulling it down and putting up a guest house for his business friends in its place. But the visit proved to be the beginning of a very fine friendship. The initiative was taken by Mrs. Duara. An Austrian by birth, she met her husband in war-time London, and has lived in India for over thirty years. She is kindly and generous, and she is more. Cast in the *grande dame* tradition she is the uncrowned queen of Shillong's social world. All newcomers to that city have cause to be grateful to her, for it is she who first invites them to a meal and makes them feel welcome. There is no one whom she does not know, no one in whose welfare she is not interested. One meets the most interesting people of the entire north-east in her beautiful drawing room, which has perhaps the loveliest view of any room in Shillong, the most cheerful fireplace, and the most comfortable sofas. Later, in the dining room, the food is equally marvelous.

Mr. Duara is the perfect gentleman. Kindly, polite, considerate, he knows exactly when a guest's glass needs replenishment, or the fire poked. Trim, handsome, always elegantly dressed, and looking at least twenty years younger than his age, he might almost be the model for the glamorized pictures of the English country squire. He stays fit by playing golf daily, whatever the weather, but he is more than just a gentleman and sportsman, being something of a Sanskrit and Assamese scholar too. His recent trip to the United States has added immensely to his fund of stories and anecdotes, which he recounts with great relish and a fine sense of the timing of the punch line. Many people have laughed with much good humor at the way that Bapu Duara traveled to New Bedford.

Bapu and Ellie Duara complement and support each other perfectly, Ellie's somewhat mercurial temperament being given a solid anchor in Bapu's good-natured sobriety, his seeming lack of spark being offset by her gaiety and energy. Together they form a beautiful and devoted couple.

Ellie Duara heard from me that Frances was in the hospital with jaundice, and decided that we needed to be taken under her wing. Her resolve was only strengthened when she discovered that Frances's father, like herself, had been born in Austria.

"Which city?" she inquired.

"Graz," I replied.

"Graz is for the bourgeoisie. I am Viennese." She went on to ask whether we had children, when Frances had felt her illness coming on, what kind of a room she had been given in the hospital, who her doctor was, and what she was being given to eat. Rude questions, you might say, coming from a total stranger. But you would be doing Mrs. Duara injustice. You should get down to brass tacks immediately; certain things about people *have* to be known if you are going to establish any relationship with them; and it is much easier in the long run to elicit this information through half a dozen sharp, pointed questions than have to garner it over a period of time through oblique hints, half-correct guesses, and gossip with third parties. So Mrs. Duara continued to fire her questions, and I stood them as manfully as I could.

At length she was satisfied, except on one count.

"I do not think that the hospital is giving her the right kind of food. She should have a lot of sugar Tell the doctor that. If he objects, say that I said so; then he'll listen. I've known him since he was a boy. He did his medical degree with my son. I prescribed a high sugar diet for him when he had jaundice years ago, and he got well." She paused, then concluded, "Tomorrow I shall visit Frances myself, and I shall bring along for her a jar of home-made jam. I hope she speaks German. It's been a long time since I spoke any, and I would like to get it back into shape again."

The visit took place, and the jam, of which I ate the better part—I've already told you how hospital food kept me alive in those days—proved delicious. It was made of a local fruit called *sohyong*, which means, literally, the black fruit, and bore a distinct resemblance to the damson plum. More important,

Frances and Ellie approved of each other, though Ellie thought that Frances's German was deplorable and not at all what one would hear in Vienna. The visit concluded with an invitation to dinner once Frances was out of the hospital.

It was at this dinner that we met the Rustomjis. Most of those who read what I am writing are likely to have met Nari Rustomji or at least to have heard of him; some of them may even be familiar with his two enchanting books on India's north-eastern borderlands and the Dragon Kingdom of Bhutan. Indeed, Nari Rustomji is famous—so famous, in fact, that as Frances once quipped, Cambridge has invited him to spend a year there, not so that he might study or research a project, but so that other scholars may study him. He is well worth this attention. Among the ICSs of recent vintage, he must be unique in that he spent his entire service career in in one part of India, and neither sought nor was invited to hold important posts in New Delhi. Scholar, musician, gymnast, author, administrator, bird watcher, wildlife lover: Nari was a far more humane, interesting, cultured and genuine person than anyone in NEHU. What we loved him for above all these qualities, however, was his deep and real commitment to people as people—and to all kinds of people. His friends ranged from the exalted personages of his day to the headhunters of Nagaland. He knew the sweepers, the laborers, the porters of Shillong as he knew governors and chief ministers.

And he loved the sweepers, the laborers and porters more. Though he was Chief Secretary of Meghalaya, and one of the most senior civil servants in India, it quite often happened that someone would walk into his office for a small loan, or seek his help in getting accommodation for a night or two in the tourist hostel. On one occasion a foreign couple was imprisoned by the government for overstaying their permit, and they created a bit of a fuss in jail. Mr. Rustomji heard of the incident, decided that the couple were well worth getting to know, and was at the jail gate when they were released. As soon as they came out, he put them into his car and drove them home for lunch and a chat! He was equally concerned with the welfare of animals in the small zoo in Shillong—indeed, the zoo is largely his creation. It houses, among other animals, a slow loris, which is nocturnal. I once mentioned to him that the creature was looking rather sick, to which he replied that it became active at night, and had I ever seen it then? When I said I hadn't, he at once arranged to take me to see the loris at midnight, when, he assured me, it looked anything but sick.

Civil servants like Nari Rustomji are rare in India today, and surely the loss is India's. With a fantastically complicated bureaucratic system, huge sums of money being spent on developmental projects, and a multitude of incomprehensible social, political and economic factors operating on the national life at all levels, it is perhaps understandable if the average civil servant loses her or his sense of individuals as individuals and becomes wrapped up in theories, models, and concepts of impersonal historical forces at work. That Mr. Rustomji knew about these forces is abundantly clear from the nature of the difficult and delicate assignments he held during his career, as also from his books. But as a civil servant he knew also something that the average bureaucrat doesn't. He knew that systems, forces, theories and models are ultimately for the people, not people for them. For all that he was Chief Secretary of a strategic State with unstable and rather volatile politics, it was the individual citizen that he served first and last. Was there a poor woman in the clutches of a moneylender? Had someone been constantly billed wrongly by the Electricity department? Was there a blind turning that caused accidents? Had garbage not been cleared from a certain area? Was there a leak in the roof of a bus station? Nari Rustomji was quite capable of bringing the whole weight of his office, and of the entire government machinery under his command, to bear on the problem. His detractors—and there are some— charge him with being concerned with trivia. Where are the statistics and the wall charts, they ask; what do the figures reveal? How many schemes were started last year? Yet the fact remains that the quality of life in Shillong and, in fact, the whole of Meghalaya, is richer, and many people who might have been unhappy are happier, because Nari Rustomji came into their lives, while schemes are started every year but several of them involve making water flow from valleys up to hilltops, and no one is appreciably better off for them.

Nari has, together with this concern for individuals, another wholly lovable attribute. He is totally eccentric; I may even say that in the best sense of the word he is totally mad. Shortly after we first got to know him, we were surprised one day to find him driving up to our house with his family. We were even more surprised when we discovered that he had dressed up for the "expedition" in some kind of a safari suit, sun hat, walking stick, goggles and binoculars. Only a water bottle was wanting. I couldn't help exclaiming, as I went up to greet him, "Dr. Livingstone, I presume." The fact that he had just decided to drop in to say hello is indication enough of his informal and friendly approach to people of all classes and conditions. But what I most want to draw attention to was his garb, which could be quite *outre* at times. He has, on various occasions, affected the Sikkimese dress, the Naga shawl, and a bleeding Madras jacket. Even when dressed in a sober looking suit of unmistakably English cut, there is something a bit unusual: the trousers seem to be tied not around his waist but come up almost to his chest, in the approved fashion of the 1930s and 40s.

This unusual style of dressing is symptomatic of pleasing little eccentricities in other areas as well. He would hardly ever sit in a chair, preferring to squat on the floor with his shoes off. At official functions he would often refuse to take his place with dignitaries in the front row and sit at the back instead, where he could talk to students and other ordinary people rather than dull officials. But my fondest memory of him is the time he visited us one evening with his gracious and lovely wife Avi and his even madder elder brother Minoo. We talked about this and that with great animation, and then suddenly he asked Frances and me, "Have you ever seen me standing on my head?"

"I've seen you do nothing else," said Avi.

"No, but really, would you like me to stand on my head?" he persisted.

Minoo looked a bit apprehensive, but we could only give one answer to his question. Thereupon, quick as lightning, he kicked off his shoes and performed a perfect *shirshasan* on our living room carpet. Minoo, not to be outdone, went into a contorted yogic posture, while Avi continued to talk to us as though nothing had happened. From time to time, Minoo joined the conversation in spite of the fact that his toes were above his head, while Nari claimed that the world looked much better from his upside down position. Two rare birds and one perfect Avi!

India's north-east has had the singular good fortune of being served by some of its finest administrators and most cultivated men, and we had the inestimable privilege of numbering some of them among our friends. Mr. Rustomji was one; another, and a very different type of person, was Mr. L. P. Singh, the governor the north-east States of Assam, Meghalaya, Nagaland, Manipur and Tripura. I had taught his son in Delhi, and his daughter was the magistrate who had married Frances and me; and I suppose it was because Mr. Singh heard of one or both these facts that we got an invitation to visit him. The card simply said that the Governor would be at home to us at a quarter to seven in the evening. We had never met any governors before or been to a Raj Bhawan, and didn't know what to expect. So I took my one and only suit out of mothballs and had it pressed, while Frances put on her best *sari*. At a quarter to seven we were stopped at the gates of Raj Bhawan, where we mentioned our names, and I overheard a quick phone call being put through to the main building. Two minutes later, having parked my scooter (a rather plebian, not to say ludicrous way to arrive at Raj Bhawan), we were ushered into an enormous drawing room. Shortly thereafter, the Governor entered.

Frankly, I was awed, and never quite managed to shake off this feeling, though I got to know him well. My first impression was that Mr. Singh was an enormously tall man, the tallest man I had seen in the north-east. Later, I was to discover that he was the tallest man in the north-east in more than just a physical sense. He is a man of great dignity and some reserve, but he is also a very kind man, correct in his behavior but affable and polite, and with a sense of humor. His wife is more capable of putting people at ease, and has a greater fund of small talk. But this should not deceive anyone into thinking that she is intellectually softer. She is, in fact, every bit his equal in the quality of mind, width of culture, and range of knowledge and experience. She is also what her husband, because of his official position, cannot afford to be: outspoken. When Morarji Desai made his first official visit to Shillong as Prime Minister, the Raj Bhawan hosted a dinner in his honor to which a large number of people were invited. At one point during the meal the Prime Minister, who was eating his usual diet of dried fruits and nuts, asked his hostess if other guests were being served the same fare. "Of course not," Mrs. Singh shot back. "I can't afford to feed them what I have to feed you."

My first meeting with the governor began in a rather stiff and formal way, with he and I making small, inconsequential talk over scotch, while Frances and Mrs. Singh got on somewhat better over a fine Napoleon brandy. And then suddenly there was a patter of feet, and a little girl came running in. I have seldom seen such a transformation. The governor's stiffness disappeared, his face shone, his eyes sparkled, and a childlike pleasure suffused his whole being as he gathered up his only grandchild in his arms and seated her in his lap. The girl, it appears, was the daughter of the magistrate who had married Frances and me. When that had happened, the magistrate herself was single. But perhaps inspired by our example, she had proceeded to get married herself shortly afterwards, and then gone ahead of us by having a child. This child was the apple of her grandfather the governor's eye.

Her arrival naturally led the conversation to subjects such as the family, domestic responsibilities, and so on, and imperceptibly the four grown-ups sitting in one corner of an overbearingly large room developed a rapport. The evening ended much more enjoyably than it had begun, and we left with the feeling that a kind of friendship based on mutual respect was possible, but that it would have to be a friendship within certain unmentioned but clearly understood perimeters.

Time bore this out. We never became fully informal in the Singhs' company. We never called them by their names. To me he was always "Sir," and to the more democratically minded Frances, nothing. ("Mr. Singh" would have sounded rude, and she never calls anyone "Sir"). We never invited them to visit us, and protocol wouldn't have allowed it. We never "dropped in" for an evening of casual chat. We went only when we were invited, but with the passage of time these invitations became more frequent, and we dropped the practice of sitting in the big drawing room. One cold winter night we were ushered into their bedroom where a fire was burning, and the atmosphere was altogether more cosy and informal, Thereafter, this is where we would meet. On occasion we would stay on to supper in their private dining room. And, of course, when their children were with them there would be much more noise and laughter, and the dogs would come in and jump all over us, and the Raj Bhawan waiters would be less unbending and even smile as they served us.

There was another small, subtle sign that I was pleased to notice. The Governor, on his own admission, has two whiskies every night, not more, and they are measured out carefully by Mrs. Singh herself. After our first couple of visits, I noticed that he would join me in a third, usually making a little joke as he did so. Conversation also became more limber. I find that when in the presence of a man of such massive intellect, enormous abilities, and vast experience, it is better to listen than to express half-baked opinions or slick comments. The result was that at our meetings he did most of the talking. But the talk now flowed naturally and easily over a great range: military history, the latest Saul Bellow novel, universities in India fifty years ago, Harvard today, the wood carvings of Gujarat, Mrs. Gandhi's place in history, philosophical speculations, methodologies for the anthropological study of north-eastern tribes. Only one subject was taboo—NEHU. We talked about it in general terms, but I thought it improper to discuss it in any detail, and Mr. Singh never pumped me on the subject, which is just as well, for he was Chief Rector of the university and it would have been quite wrong to discuss its affairs with him at these informal get togethers.

Mr. Rustomji is a serving officer of the ICS; Mr. L.P. Singh is a retired officer. Unlike Mr. Rustomji, who has spent his whole career serving in the north-east, Mr. Singh was Home Secretary to the government of India before he was appointed governor. Unlike Nari Rustomji, who is interested above all in individuals, L.P. Singh is interested in the forces that drive and govern people in societies. His sweep of vision is vast, historical, and impersonal. He is concerned with history: with understanding to a nicety why things happen the way they do, and the extent to which individuals may mold the course of events. While Nari reads all kinds of things, L.P. Singh reads mostly history, and is interested in fiction only to the extent that it helps understand and interpret human motivations. Having worked all his life in very close connection with politicians, though he himself has no political ambitions himself, L.P. Singh understands the mind of the manipulator of men, and understands, too, the dangers inherent in this manipulation. Nari, for all his experience, is an incorrigible believer in the goodness of men; L.P. Singh understands, too well that men can suffer from cupidity and this can make them false. I always found him eloquent on this subject and marveled at the man who, himself the model of the most upright integrity, found himself dealing daily with dishonest politicians of all kinds.

It was not through them, however, that he saw himself performing his real work in the north-east.

He often said that the three tasks he had set before himself when he became governor were the settlement of the Naga problem, the establishment of the North East Council (NEC), and putting NEHU along the right lines of development. Each of these tasks, it will be noticed, had to do with issues and institutions and history; success would benefit individuals, but for him the individual *per se* was part of larger issues and tensions. Success would also bring about historical change: history, then, could be made through the right use of institutions. Moreover, these institutions required a certain type of man or woman to work them, and would, in turn, create a certain kind of man or woman. The ideal worker was not going to be one who sought change through manipulating people— the politician—but one who sought change by nursing institutions and values—the professional, be he or she teacher, doctor, lawyer, civil servant, what have you. Hence, though he understood the politician's mind, and spent his life working with them, it was to people of some vision or dedication or ideals and professional competence that he turned for companionship. My most vivid memory of him is standing on the porch of Raj Bhawan one night, bidding good night to a few people he had invited. Besides Frances and myself there were Mrinal and Sujata Miri (colleagues, friends and members of the Philosophy department), an economist with the North East Council, and one or two others. Sujata the irrepressible had been particularly lively and full of fun that evening. She had kept us all amused with jokes directed at herself. Now, as she was getting her very ample self into a car, she said, "Governor Sahib, I am so fat because I am a glutton and eat a lot."

"Sujata," smiled the Governor, "Dante says that the glutton seeks God through his gluttony. You must be in search of something."

This, it has always seemed to me, sums up L.P. Singh well: he has a sense of humor, but there is a serious point to it. The ability to quote Dante speaks of his wide reading, his standing on the porch to see his guests off of his courtesy and politeness, the kind of people he was seeing off to his belief in the values and talents by which history can be made. Austere, erect, just; but the human being underneath flashes into view in the face of an incongruous situation and reveals a mind aware of the heritage of the past and conscious of man's quest for something bigger than the self.

Every inch a Governor. Often, as I passed Raj Bhawan, I used to say to myself that so long as L.P. Singh was living there, all would be well with the north-east.

One of the glories of Shillong is that it shelters an uncommonly large number of odd-bods, cranks, eccentrics and otherwise colorful personalities. We got to know several, and loved them all. I have already mentioned Mr. Booth and Mr. Rustomji, but there were others. Swarup Mukerjee, the son of an ex-Prime Minister of Baroda State, and with an Oxford degree in Geography, had given up a lucrative job with the Inland River Navigation system to start a small, hippie-type eating joint in Shillong, called Simrit, or "little bird." On a typical evening you were likely to encounter there a Deputy Inspector General or Superintendent of Police, maybe a government Secretary or two, the odd businessman, one or two NEHU professors, a handful of college students, and some respectable and not so respectable citizens, all doing justice to the *chow* or chops. Students, in particular, love Swarup. His food is a welcome change from the hostel routine, and he is always kind with credit to those who have not received money from home. But what makes it fun to eat in Simrit is the pleasure of his conversation, which is always witty and urbane. *Bon mots* and shrewd comments on men and affairs are uttered in impeccable English, while sounds and smells of very un-English cooking come from the kitchen next door.

Mr. Richmond speaks impeccable English too. He should: he was born in the Border country, the son of a parish priest. For about forty years he planted tea in Assam, fished and shot in every stream and every forest, and realized that if he wanted to enjoy the good things of life like sausages and beer, he had better learn to make them himself. He learnt those skills so well, in fact, that after retirement he settled down in Shillong to make sausages and other pork products, which now have a ready market in a good deal of north-east India. Buying a ham from him is not just a business transaction. It involves being introduced to Zippo, a glorious and lazy labrador, and then you share a bottle of beer with the dog and his owner, while the latter fills you up on all the local gossip, peppering his conversation with jokes and good-natured but astringent remarks on "those Khasis." (Mr. Richmond is particularly qualified to talk about the Khasis, having married one of their finest specimens years ago, and lived with her in perfect bliss ever since). After you have drained your glass of beer, the conversation turns to Assam as it was before Independence, and then to local politics. Then the ham you came to buy is wrapped up and handed over, and Mr. Richmond gloats over how he has imported a syringe with which he can inject a ham with water in such a way that he can sell the same amount of meat at twice its weight and therefore twice its price. You go home and, fearing that you have been one of his business victims, you undo the parcel. The ham is excellent, and, as a bonus for having drunk beer with Zippo, he has given you a packet of sausages as well.

Surely V. S. ("Hari") Jaffa and his wife Jyoti belong to this group of lovable and generous eccentrics. I have always thought that it was in the fitness of things that we should have been introduced by Mr. Booth. "What, you haven't met the Jafas even *once!*" he exclaimed incredulously one day. "In that case, permit me to take you to their house immediately." Hari proved to be an enormous man with a wide grin and an ingratiating, bear-like manner; Jyoti was small and boyish. They were dressed in riding breeches, having just returned from a brisk ten-mile ride. Drinks were produced, and in no time the atmosphere became jovial and lively. Hari brought out his accordion (a fit instrument for a man his size, I've always thought) and played soulful melodies, while Jyoti talked enchantingly about her childhood in Rajasthan, their years in Mizoram, and miniature painting. I came away in love with them.

We saw them frequently thereafter. They were always welcome. Hari came on a bit strong at times. "Frances!" he would holler as soon as he arrived, "I want omelettes for dinner, and stuff them properly with onions." While Frances busied herself in the kitchen, Jyoti would announce that she never went near so plebeian a place, and then, putting on her best schoolgirl manner and accent, ask, "Could I please have a glass of milk?" In the meanwhile, Hari was rousing the neighbors with his accordion music. At about midnight he would decide that he wanted a smoke, and we would walk down to a cigarette shop not far away. Finding it shut, and the owner fast asleep inside, Hari would start battering at the door. Once the police constable on duty woke up sooner than the shopkeeper and came to investigate, but finding that it was only Mr. Jafa wanting to buy a packet of cigarettes, he saluted smartly and wished us a polite good night. Policemen—indeed, everyone in Shillong—adored Hari. After Mr. Booth he had been probably the most popular Deputy Commissioner of Shillong, and was currently being a great success as Director of Education.

Boisterousness, high spirits, rough fun—these are certainly part of his character. But let us not be fooled into thinking that Hari is just an overgrown schoolboy. Underneath he is sensitive, and very gentle. He has tact, and, like Nari Rustomji, a real sympathy for people. Like Nari again, he belongs to a vanishing breed of civil servants, one who is wedded to the welfare of people, not to causes or ambition. It was not in his office that he did his best work but out in the field, around village campfires, or in remote and hilly tracts, sharing the simple life of the mountain dwellers.

Jyoti is one of the most complex people I have known. Born in a noble Rajput family, she never forgets this fact, nor does she allow other middle-class urbanites to forget it. But it gives her a real rapport with the poor, the underprivileged or the deprived, towards whom she shows invariably the most perfect politeness and consideration. She was being trained as a foreign service officer when she met Hari, who was being trained as an IAS officer, and for his sake she sacrificed what promised to be a brilliant diplomatic career. But talent cannot be suppressed; and when we first met, she was about to publish, with Writer's Workshop, Calcutta, her first novel, a historical romance set in the reign of Jahangir. She could be vivacious, snobbish, sympathetic, catty, polite, morose, all within minutes. She prided herself on being an excellent shot, and so we were all very relieved when she tried to put a bullet in her brain one morning and missed, the bullet lodging in a bone in her nose instead. We were all at her bedside when she regained consciousness after surgery. On seeing us standing, her first reaction was to stand up too, as good manners demanded; and finding she could not do that, her attitude changed to one of concern for our comfort as she cast her eyes around the room to make sure there were enough chairs for us.

It is sad to think that such a fine woman is currently finding it difficult to live with all her complexities. Nothing that she does will surprise me, though: for Jyoti, life would be dull indeed if she ever settled into a predictable routine. Ultimately, it is this openness to every kind of possibility that has always made her so valuable to friends.

Shekhar Singh merits a mention too. He was a student of philosophy at St. Stephen's, Delhi, and after his M.A. was appointed lecturer there. He, too, ended up in Shillong as a lecturer in the philosophy department. He was single and needed a place to live; and since we were not using the cottage on our property that Mr. Booth had given us, we asked him to move in and pay Mr. Booth the rent. Later his mother came to live with him, whereupon Mr. Booth, in his typical fashion, extended the cottage by constructing two more bedrooms and bathrooms, so that what was originally a small cottage now became quite a spacious house while still retaining its attractive cottage-like appearance from the outside, complete with the beautiful climbing rose.

Since Shekhar was our immediate neighbor, he would sometimes have his meals with us, and there was always much to discuss. Soon, however, the Vice Chancellor singled him out for special favors. Shekhar was made in charge of various plans and projects, and a jeep was put at his disposal. This brought him closer to some people, like Towcchaung, the Officer on Special Duty for Administration and, in some ways, the most powerful man in the university (more about him later) because Towcchaung liked to go hunting, and the jeep was just the right conveyance for that purpose. When a bigwig in the university became dependent on Shekhar's favors, it added to Shekhar's stature in the university. It also caused a lot of resentment. People began to think that he was getting to be too big for his boots. Not the women students, however. Shekhar was a favorite of theirs. They would often come to his cottage, hardly a cottage any more, and hold parties and singalongs. We, being right next door, couldn't help being aware of all these goings on. Not that we minded: it wasn't our business, and nothing illegal was being done. People were just having a good time. But it also meant that we pulled a little apart from Shekhar.

We were not part of his young crowd, nor were we part of the top brass of the university with whom he was becoming closer. So though we remained collegial and friendly, the relationship never developed as closely as I had originally expected.

Noorul introduced us to Brother Brendan McCartheigh, and we became friends. It was one of the few friendships that continued well beyond our Shillong years. Brendan was an Irishman, and a member of the Christian Brothers, an Irish religious order that focuses on school teaching, and he worked at St. Edmund's College, one of the only two colleges that the Christian Brothers run, the other being Iona College in New Rochelle, just outside New York City. We would drop in to see Brendan fairly frequently, enjoy the large hot cups of tea he served, admire a beautiful tree with yellow blossoms from his window, and talk about everything we could think of. He is a deeply religious man who has made India his home and is deeply committed to its youth, their mental and psychic welfare, and to the growth and development of the country. A man of wide interests with an open, questing, questioning mind, he likes to promote these qualities in his charges, but is very careful to see that their mental and psychological equilibrium remains stable and they remain focused on their goals. Pedagogical methods were a very frequent topic of our discussions, as were exams and the tremendous pressure they impose on students. What came through was his concern not only with the intellectual but also the inner lives of his students and their ability to cope with stress, their psychological well-being. We would bring him up to date on the affairs of NEHU in which he took a suitably distanced interest, and exchange news of the people we knew. Brendan played the clarinet, and on a trip back home to Ireland busked for a buck or two in the London underground. He did not play for us, but would do so for his students and in various social and cultural programs that the college organized. We were sorry to say good bye to him when we finally left Shillong.

How we got to know Mr. Thorose, I cannot now recall; probably it was through Mr. Booth. The Thorose are an Armenian family and have lived in India for generations, as have so many other Armenians. The paterfamilias was now retired, but had worked for many years in Calcutta for the Ford Motor Company. He would regale us with stories over the most delicious dinners of the way the company imported cars from Detroit, fitted them for Indian conditions, including changing the drive from the left to the right side, and then sent them off to various parts of the country to be sold. My father used to have a V8 Ford of the 1938 model, and Mr. Thorose would sometimes try to recall how many such cars had been imported and where they had been sold. From him you could learn about the different makes and models of Ford cars, and the far worse quality and inflated prices of contemporary

Indian cars like the ubiquitous Ambassador. He was also very informative on Armenian history and the story of their presence in India. The Thoroses were delightful company, and we always enjoyed our meetings and conversations.

One of the more rewarding aspects of a teacher's life is that his work results naturally in friendships with students. We were very fond of our students who represented all the people of the north-east, the Assamese, the Khasis, the Garos, the Jaintias, the Nagas of various sub-tribes, the Mizos, and people from Arunachal Pradesh. The Khasis were in a majority since the university is located in Shillong, but the other tribes and regions were well represented. We were always glad to see them, in the classroom and in our home or theirs. However, we found that, because of the rather restricted lives they led, the rather oppressive atmosphere of the colleges they had attended, and the fact that the north-east was rather cut off from the rest of India, their horizons were somewhat limited and their curiosity unawakened. Yet they were as charming, open, frank and friendly young men and women as could be found anywhere in the world. They did not exhibit in any striking manner the ability to plough their own lonely furrows, or think about life in novel terms. But they were perfectly happy in their environment and fully adjusted to it. None suffered from any trauma or insecurity, none showed in any marked degree a desire to kick against authority. This made them uninteresting sometimes, but always pleasant. They needed to be led by the hand and wanted that some older person should open their eyes to the wonder of the world. I found their lack of guile and their faith in their teachers most touching.

In my first year at NEHU I started weekly poetry reading sessions at our house. Students would sit around informally, have tea and snacks, and read, or hear other people read, poetry out aloud. Students came regularly, but I soon found the what interested them more was not poetry but general conversation, and so these sessions turned into at-homes. Students loved our pets, would advise us on the garden, and were quite happy to do the washing up after they had had tea. Sometimes a few students who lived in the hostel would use our kitchen to cook a north-eastern delicacy that their tribe was particularly fond of; and this proved to be an excellent introduction to the cuisine of the area. And one year we were overwhelmed by their spontaneous kindness. We had invited them to tea on our wedding anniversary, and they came laden with gifts. I do not, as a rule, accept presents from students, but this time it was impossible to say no. In future years, though we continued to invite them on our anniversary, we also made it absolutely clear that they were not to bring presents. That did not prevent them from giving us expensive greetings cards. They did this spontaneously because they wanted to share our joy, rather than with any calculated motive. I don't know how much we taught them, but we certainly learned from our student friends, and perhaps the most valuable lesson we learned was how to enjoy life, and be simple, unaffected, and happy. They may not have been the world's greatest students, though three or four of them were as good as any I have ever taught, and one or two went on to distinguish themselves in the academic world outside India. Several lacked ambition, drive, or discipline. The casual, lackadaisical attitude towards work on the part of a few could irritate and annoy me. But they were all, truly, beautiful people.

If my reader has got so far, she or he may well wonder why, though I have talked of our friends drawn from the professional class of the plains Indians, I have said nothing about friendships with tribal people of the same class. Is it, they may ask, because we made no tribal friends? We did get to know and to like several middle-class and educated Khasis, mostly of the older generation, like Queenie Rynjah, the now retired headmistress of a prestigious girls' school which she ran with great efficiency, and her husband, with whom I served on the governing body of a local women's college. But these exceptions apart, the truth is that we made very few friends from among the professional and administrative class of Khasis. There are a large number of such people in Shillong. There are Khasi doctors, engineers, lawyers, scientists, civil servants; but a majority of the people manning these posts were, until recently, Bengalis, Assamese, and other "outsiders." Now Khasis are replacing them; but many of these Khasis tend to be provincial and limited in their outlook. We found them, by and large, uninspiring and uninteresting. Some tended to be on the defensive and gave the impression that they suffered from a chip on their shoulders about being Khasis; others were smug and happy-go-lucky in their attitudes, or else unduly full of expressions such as "We Khasis," and insisted that theirs was a great society which others couldn't understand. Now all these attitudes are perfectly understandable when you consider the cultural isolation of the north-east and the exploitation of the Khasis by outsiders until recently. But they don't conduce to natural friendships. Even the so-called "leaders" of society were either unduly prickly about their culture or else talked at length about it without knowing much of what they were talking about. When you asked them how old a particular monument was, they could only reply that it was very old; when you asked them to explain some phenomenon of Khasi society, they could only tell you what you already knew. I found, after a good deal of persistent probing, that their minds were, for the most part, empty, and some of their attitudes revolting.

I'll give two instances. For political and other reasons, a certain leading politician was a frequent visitor to the English department. He was supposed to be a great scholar and an authority on local history and folklore, but I never heard him talk of anything but himself. Once, when addressing students, he divided his talk into two parts. The first part was how NEHU was for the tribals of the north-east— which was largely true—and, in special, for the Khasis—which was not true. As such, he declared that "foreigners and outsiders" had no real place in the set-up. It might have been a good vote-winning sentiment (though he lost the election held shortly afterwards), but it seemed to me that to thus restrict the scope and vision of a central university in what was meant to be a thoughtful speech to thoughtful students was to strike a blow at the very concept of a university.

The second part was about himself. We were told how he was always being chosen to attend international conferences, and how at the last one he attended he had spoken on as many as seven subjects, while other participants had been able to speak on not more than three. The speech ended by our being told that he had been congratulated by several foreigners on his performance.

Here was a contradiction indeed. I couldn't understand why, on the one hand, he wanted to do away with "foreigners and outsiders," and on the other made it a point to mention that he had been praised by foreigners. Nor could I see how it was ever possible to be friends with him.

My second illustration concerns a person it was Frances's misfortune to have to deal with once every year. Let me explain. Since the days of the British, Shillong has been a restricted area, which means that foreigners have required special permission to live there. Since Frances is an American national, she had to apply for a renewal of her permit yearly. The man in charge always tried to be polite, but every time we went to his office we were struck by his obnoxious attitudes, though he was perhaps quite unconscious of the effect he was producing.

On one occasion Frances was going to the New York to visit her parents, and the gentleman asked her to bring back half a dozen fishing floats. For those who know anything about it, these floats are small, cheap and light; and since the request wasn't all that difficult to fulfill, Frances was glad to oblige. She got the floats from a fishing store in New York, where the storekeeper informed her that the person she was buying them for must be a very mediocre fisherman, for good fishermen had stopped using them the world over many years ago.

When Frances returned, she went to see this gentleman with the floats. He was pleased to receive them, thanked her profusely, expressed a desire to be friends with us, and invited us home to tea. We were delighted. But imagine Frances's mortification when the only subject he talked about for two hours was what a dreadful race of people the Americans are, and how he was a good fisherman, and no American he had ever met knew the first thing about fishing.

I am prepared to grant that he was a good fisherman (though Mr. Booth, who knows about these things, doesn't think so). I am also prepared to grant that a man has a perfect right to praise himself in his own home. I may perhaps even go so far as to grant that perhaps he was right that Americans are dreadful people. But surely you don't invite an American who has done you a favor to your house, and then proceed to tell her all this.

No, friendship was ruled out with people of this kind. Fortunately, however, we soon discovered that the middle class, educated, professional Khasi did not always or necessarily represent the best in his society. There was a whole lot of other people too, the office clerk, the carpenter, the domestic servant, the housewife, the vegetable seller, the cleaner or charwoman; and though they had no intellectual or cultural pretensions, they had no complexes either. They were simple if limited people, but they responded warmly to people and situations, and we found ourselves responding warmly to them. They lived all around us, and many of them became our friends. It was through them that we came to understand and appreciate the best features of Khasi society.

I doubt, though, whether we should have been able to make so many friends among our neighbors, and been accepted by them so fully, had it not been for our *kongs*. The word *kong* in Khasi means sister; it is the usual appellation for women, and, in particular, this is how Khasi domestic workers are addressed. These workers, or *kongs*, are unlike any other Indian maids. They do not regard themselves as servants, and you would be unwise to regard them thus. Instead, they see themselves as your helpers: they will help you in your domestic chores, but they consider themselves every bit your equals, and as good as you are. So long as you treat them in this manner, all will be well. But woe to the family that shouts at a *kong* or talks to her in a way in which north Indian families generally behave towards servants. One of my neighbors, a Punjabi family, had any amount of trouble with their *kongs*. No girl would work for them for any length of time; finally, Khasi women stopped working for them altogether. The reason was simple. The lady of the house had always bossed her servants around, and when she tried to do the same with her *kongs*, they simply walked out. One of these girls, a friend of ours, told us later that she wasn't going to stand being treated like a servant, and her parting words to her erstwhile employer had been, "You're not good enough for me, you, you—Punjabi!"

Two days after we had settled into Arden, there was a knock at the door, and we found a young woman of twenty or twenty one standing there. She giggled a lot, and sounded rather incoherent, but finally we gathered that she wanted to "help" us. Frances was still not fully recovered, and we needed someone to do the housework. So, on the spur of the moment, and without knowing the first thing about the girl at the door, we agreed to hire her for fifty rupees a month, which was the figure she mentioned.

Her name was Between. Khasi names can be peculiar, and I shall have more to say about them later, but we thought that Between was a bit extreme, till she explained that she was a twin, and the word *Be* in Khasi means "little girl." As a child she was, naturally enough, called Be twin, and over the years Between had become her established name. She was solid, hard-working, reliable and cheerful. We reposed the fullest trust in her. She would sometimes take as many as a hundred rupees from us when she went shopping, but always rendered meticulous accounts. She had her own key to the house, and would come and go as and when she pleased, but we knew that nothing would ever be stolen. She kept the house spotlessly clean, and it was a pleasure to smell the clean, fresh smell the house seemed to exude after she had done her job with broom and brush. She was Frances's friend and companion, and from her we learnt a good deal not only about where to shop, or how floors were polished, but also about our neighbors, and about working-class Khasi life generally. She also provided us with our most intimate glimpses of Khasi village life. She was a village girl herself, and once invited Frances to her village. Frances met all the ramifications of the family, was taken out boating on the river, and made much of a fuss over. Later, owing to a paucity of beds in the family, she shared Between's bed for the night. On a later occasion I, too, spent a couple of nights in her village and enjoyed myself hugely, except that I was not accorded the pleasure of sharing Between's bed.

If Between had faults, they lay largely in her talents as a cook. A simple village girl, her idea of a typical meal was a bit of boiled meat and a boiled vegetable, to be eaten with boiled rice. When she saw Frances's spice cabinet, she went wild and we were served the most inedible dishes in which heaps of turmeric mingled most infelicitously with fistfuls of thyme. Finally, we had to put our foot down, and thereafter it was boiled rice and vegetables during all the time that Between remained with us.

Another fault she shared with many other Khasis. They are, as I have said, very house proud, and clean, shine and polish with great gusto. But they seem to be averse to a removal of cobwebs. Maybe it is because many of them are short – and, being unable to reach the cobwebs, prefer to leave them alone. Whatever the reason, the fact remains that neither Between nor her successors would remove cobwebs from the ceiling and the walls until we absolutely pestered them to do so. Finally, Frances and I agreed that removing cobwebs was not too much work for us, considering how much Between managed herself.

At first, she came to work alone; soon, however, her two-year old daughter Percy, and her dog Lion, began to accompany her. Lion, as I mentioned earlier, finally left Between altogether and attached himself to us.

Percy never went so far, but she and we became fond of one another. She would romp around happily in the garden while Between did the house chores, or else go off to sleep quietly on the living room couch. If she saw Frances or me anywhere in the street, she would let out a high, piercing "Good morning!" irrespective of the time of day, and her cry would be heard long after we had lost sight of her. She was a good, happy, healthy child, as most Khasi children are, not afraid of strangers, and quite capable of keeping herself amused without making too many demands on her mother.

Gradually Between started inviting other friends to the house. Every day we would be introduced to a new face, Juliana or Theresa or Pristina or a rather sulky boy named Weevil, or the twins Hobble and Jobble. Sometimes, when we were not at home, Between found it more convenient to entertain her friends in our house than in her own rather cramped dwelling. Also, if any one of her friends wanted a hot bath, or had to use the telephone, she urged them to use our house as their own. Frances and I did not really mind: indeed, Between and her cohorts proved to be an excellent introduction to the people of our little neighborhood; and because we accepted their presence in our house, they accepted us also, and many were the smiles and greetings that we would encounter as we walked past their houses to work every morning. Frances, in particular, would be mobbed by little children crying "Hey, Mem! Hey, Mem!" and rushing to be patted on the head, while rising above this din were the shrill, piercing "good mornings" of Percy. Between's cohorts also behaved well on the whole. They were friendly, vivacious, full of laughter and song and practical jokes and high spirits, and the girls were generally pretty and nice to flirt with. Though they foregathered in our house, they never made it messy, and always helped Between in her work. They would not even so much as help themselves to a cup of tea without first asking our permission.

But things changed once Between got herself a boyfriend and he started coming regularly to the house with her. He was handy around the place in more senses than one. If he knew how to repair a broken handle, for instance, he knew also how to help himself to a bit of loose change lying on the dressing table, or to the bottle of whisky in the cupboard. On one occasion some clothes disappeared, and on another, some of Frances's jewelry. When asked, Between confessed ignorance, and even now I think that she was not feigning. She was, in fact, genuinely ignorant of her boyfriend's habits. Our warning her against him produced no results, and we would have been constrained to ask her to stop working for us had she not got a job as a cleaner in the university. It was a good job, carried a respectable salary with annual increments and a paid holiday. She was very glad to take it, and so were we. We parted the best of friends.

She had barely quit when again there was a knock at the door. The young lady standing there was Balarica. She was a matriculate, and married, and spoke good English. Her ambition was to be a schoolteacher; in the meanwhile, however, the school she had set her heart on had no vacancies, and she wanted money. Did we want her to "help" us? Yes, we did, and so she moved into Between's place.

Balarica was more suspicious where Between had been open. She was a loner where Between was gregarious. She welcomed no one to the house, and was always warning us against various people, all of whom, it appeared, were housebreakers, rapists, and worse. She kept the house clean enough, though being physically weaker than Between, she couldn't brush and polish with the same vim and vigor. Where she won hands down was as a cook. She was happiest when in the kitchen, and produced the most delicious meals. Compliments made her attain even greater heights; and during the one year she was with us, we ate very well indeed.

We had joined a Khasi class so as to pick up the rudiments of the language; and when Balarica discovered this, her schoolmarmish instincts came to the fore. She would supervise our homework, sometimes doing it for us, supplement classroom lessons, and give us conversation practice. Not that we learned much Khasi, but what little we did pick up was more due to her efforts than those of our teachers.

At last a vacancy occurred in the school of her choice. I took my suit out of mothballs, and Frances put on her best *sari*. Balarica was resplendent in a *jainsem*, her hair specially done for the occasion. Together we marched down to the school and asked to see the headmistress. We introduced ourselves in impressive tones, and she was suitably impressed. We then praised her and her school, and commiserated with the lot of school teachers. The stern heart of the headmistress softened. We then introduced Balarica. "Our dear friend Mrs. Lyngdoh," I think I called her, and told the headmistress what a wonderful person she was. The headmistress saw no reason to disagree. Thereupon we suggested that any sensible headmistress would hire her straight away, and that we should have done so ourselves, but alas, we did not run a school. The ploy worked. Balarica got the job, though when it came to bargaining for the salary the headmistress proved suddenly very tough and impossible to impress. Anyway, Balarica found, at the end of the interview, that she had graduated from being a domestic help to being a lower middle-class teacher, and was going to be twenty rupees a month richer as a result. We wished her good luck and good bye: our loss was the school's gain.

So one of our *kongs* had become a government servant, Class IV, and the other a school teacher. Clearly we couldn't afford *kongs* who had high ambitions or high education. Our prayers were answered when a girl knocked at the door again. It was Dolcy, all of sixteen years of age. She combined the strength of Between with the grace and intelligence of Balarica; she was also neat, clean, shy, understanding, and artistic. She never gave us any grounds for complaint, and when, after four years in Shillong, we moved back to Delhi, she agreed to come along with us. She is now a dear and valued member of our family.

Our *kongs* were among our best friends in Shillong.

I have spoken thus far of the friends we made in Shillong. A number of our friends also came to visit us and see the Khasi Hills. I have already mentioned John Roche. He had been rather stressed just before he left Sydney on his travels, and some rather unpleasant experiences in Delhi with money changers had stressed him out more. When he came, he was wearing one black and one brown shoe because while packing in Sydney he had mixed up his pairs of shoes. He was rather embarrassed, but we assured him that no one was going to pay any attention to his feet, and in any case he could rectify the error as soon as he got to London by buying a nice pair of shoes there. The next morning Frances took him his tea, and he poured the tea in the milk jug, about which he was very apologetic. Thereafter Frances took charge of him for the week he was with us. She would do his laundry, make sure that he ate his meals properly, make his bed, and so on. Gradually he unwound and began to relax, and we hope that by the time he was ready to leave,

Shillong as well as Frances's ministrations had got him to shed much of his stress.

Noreen Dornenberg was another early visitor. She entered the Yale Graduate School to do a Ph.D. the same year that Frances and I did, in 1968. She was in the Philosophy department while we were in English, but we became friends. She was known as Sister Mary Esther then. She was training to be a nun, and had completed all her training but had yet to take her final vows, She was always immaculately turned out in a nun/s habit, and not a single hair showed through her head dress. But Yale's liberating and perhaps secularizing influence was soon at work. One day a wisp of hair could be seen on her forehead, peeping through the head dress, then a tuft. Then the nun's habit disappeared, to be replaced by a conservative dress, and finally by jeans. She went back to her original name, gave up the Order, and entered the secular world, making up for lost time. She worked as an academic for a while, but then entered the business world. She was in India to have adventure, and came to Shillong to see us. We were very happy to host her and showed her round. I like to think that she enjoyed the days she spent with us.

Then Tom and Jan Conway showed up. Jan was a good friend while I was up at Oxford. She is a world traveler. She came to see me in the United States, and here she was in Shillong, this time with her husband. Tom had been an officer in a Punjab regiment during the Second War, and recounted stories of sitting under the shade of trees on *charpoys* with Punjabi villagers, drinking *lassi*, and hearing stories of Sikandar as though he had passed through the villages only the previous week. Later he became a Trappist monk, labored in his monastery, read, prayed, and spoke to no one for twelve years. Once he left the Order he couldn't stop talking. In Shillong we would talk the whole day and into the night about all kinds of subjects, including his adventures all over the world. He was greatly interested in the culture of what he called the Kaazis (Khasis) and an Arunachal tribe called the Apatanis. It was Jan who named our puppy Romper. She (the puppy) was slow and lazy, and did not like to move much. Jan was surprised. She said that the puppy was healthy and young and should be romping about. So Kaajal was re-christened Romper, and thereafter she took to romping all over the place.

Another welcome guest was our old friend from St. Stephen's, David Baker, who taught history. Curious, energetic, fit, full of fun, often at his own expense, David was delightful company and we took him everywhere to show him the sights, and introduced him to as many people as we could. David had his ways. We would set out for a walk, and after walking about two hundred yards he would realize that there was a slight nip in the air whereas he was feeling warm at home. So we would walk back so that he could put on a sweater. Or he'd realize that the woolen socks he was wearing were not quite the right socks, so we'd return so he could change them. But we were used to his eccentricities and didn't mind; in fact, they were all part of his lovable personality. He had a good time with us, as we did with him.

One summer Rukun Advani and Vipin Handa turned up. Both had been among my best students in St. Stephen's, and I was delighted to have them over. Rukun's luggage had been stolen on the train, and the first priority therefore became to refurnish him with the things he needed for Shillong. We talked, we walked, we showed them the sights and told them stories of people and places and things. In return, they gave us news of the happenings at my old college. I like to think that they had a quiet, relaxing holiday, and that Rukun was able to get over the trauma of being robbed.

One day we were asked by the Vice Chancellor whether we would consider having Christophe van Fuhrer Heimendorf, a famous anthropoligist, over for dinner. Frances heard the name and immediately said, "Not on my life!" With a name like that, she was sure that he was a Nazi and probably even had dueling scars on his face to prove it. She herself is a New York Jew, though not religious; her father and, indeed the whole family, were evicted from their home in Austria by the Nazis and later fled to the Americas. When Devanesen had convinced her that Dr. Heimendorf was, in fact, totally opposed to Hitler and had spent the war years researching the tribes of what is now Arunachal Pradesh, she relented, but still maintained her guard when the gentleman came. But he proved to be utterly charming. He was, indeed, against the Nazis, he knew a great deal about the tribals of Arunachal and had returned after several years to study how much they had changed in the intervening years, and was wonderful raconteur of details regarding tribal life in the hills of the north east. The evening passed most pleasantly. Though he was never a house guest, he was an important visitor.

Chapter 4
THE PLACE

THE CITY OF SHILLONG IS JUST OVER A HUNDRED years old, having been founded by the Briitish in 1875. Till the 1830s the Khasis had little contact with the outside world except Assam to the north and Bengal to the south. When the British decided to enter Assam, they did so through the Khasi Hills, opening out a route first from Sylhet to Cherrapunji, and then on to Gauhati. The British entry into the Khasi Hills was to have far-reaching repercussions for the local inhabitants and for the area they inhabited.

The British found that the Khasis were organized under a number of petty and often warring Rajas. Interested in gaining the right of way through their territories, the British befriended these Rajas, often supporting them in their quarrels with one another. One Raja with whom they became particularly friendly was U Tirot Singh (the prefix U in Khasi, used for men, is an honorific, as in Burmese, e.g. U Thant), who ruled over the small kingdom of Nongkhlaw. For a number of years the relationship flourished, till Tirot

Singh, on the advice of various followers, decided to butcher a small British contingent stationed in his territory and free himself of British influence. The leader of the contingent got wind of the plan and managed to escape, but a number of British soldiers were killed. Thereafter Tirot Singh took to the hills from where he waged a guerrilla war against the British, till he was captured and imprisoned in the Dacca jail, where he died. Today he is revered as the first Khasi freedom fighter, but it is unlikely that he had any sweeping vision of national destiny and historical forces. His short-lived rebellion seems to have been inspired, rather, by a desire to rid his small principality of foreign influence; and in this limited aim, too, he seems to have been acting more on the advice of his relatives than through natural inclination.

In any case, with the capture of Tirot Singh the British became the most powerful political and military force in the Khasi Hills, and it was only a matter of time before they established themselves in Cherrapunji, which was then, and still is regarded by some as being the seat of Khasi culture.

Cherrapunji requires some description. It is famous in geography books as the place with the highest rainfall in the world, and every schoolboy or girl has heard of it. Many tourists go there, sometimes to see some quite spectacular waterfalls, a cave, a delightful oak forest, but often only to experience the rain. In quest of the last experience, they are often disappointed.

Rain in Cherrapunji, though undoubtedly heavy, feels no different from rain anywhere else; besides, it is not even a fact that Cherrapunji is the wettest place on earth. The British, in their fondness for recording and observing everything, established a small observatory in Cherrapunji when they settled there; and when they found that the average rainfall was nearly 600 inches a year, declared it to be the rainiest spot in the world, not realizing that two neighboring settlements could vie for that distinction. For the fact is that Cherrapunji is a high spot in a ridge that has two other high spots, Pynursla and Mawsynram. The clouds that form in the Bay of Bengal pass over what is now Bangladesh, meeting no obstruction till they are punctured by these three peaks on the Cherrapunji ridge. Depending on weather conditions, sometimes one of these three places gets the highest amount of precipitation, sometimes another. In 1974 I am told that Mawsynram received 1000 inches of rain, which must surely be an all-time world record.

If the world knows about Cherrapunji (or Cherra, as the Khasis call it) because of its rainfall, the Khasis themselves have a fondness for the place because of other reasons. For them, Cherra is the place from where the best bananas come, where the sweetest honey (made by bees from orange blossoms, and therefore having a faint but unmistakable orange flavor) is found, and where the purest form of Khasi is spoken. Even today a number of people in the Khasi

Hills will inform you with pride that though they have lived in Shillong or some other place for several years, their ancestors originally lived in Cherra. Though Cherra today is a small, rather ugly town whose only non-geographical boast is a somewhat damp and ill-kept Ramakrishna Mission and school, the pride with which the Khasi speaks of the town indicates the preeminent position it must have occupied in their culture and social organization in the past. No wonder, then, that when the British found themselves in a powerful political position in the Khasi Hills, they established their headquarters there, set up an observatory, and made the geographical oddity of the place famous throughout the world.

Cherra, situated as it is on a hilltop, has excellent drainage, as do most places in the Khasi Hills. The rainwater simply drains off into what is now Bangladesh, causing floods there, but leaving Cherra dry. Just how dry Cherra can be, the British found out soon enough. For the great irony is that Cherra has absolutely no source of water except the rain, and when it is not raining the town experiences acute water shortage. The obvious way to tackle the problem would have been for the British to create means of storing and conserving the rainwater. This they did not do. Instead, shortly after they had settled in Cherra, they decided to shift their headquarters away from here to a place about thirty miles distant, and across a few ridges. This new location had several advantages over

Cherra. It was closer to the Assam valley. It received less rainfall. And it had a better climate in other respects too, being cool and green all year round, and experiencing less frequently the fog and mists which are such a common feature in Cherra. So Cherra was abandoned, its acute water shortage unresolved to this day, and Shillong was established in the third quarter of the nineteenth century.

Few monuments or memorials have survived from the earliest days of British presence in the Khasi Hills. But not far from the village of Mawphlong, just over twenty miles from Shillong, is a grave that is seldom visited, and even the exact location of which is known to very few. I have never seen it myself, though I have looked for it on several occasions, but Nari Rustomji once showed me a photograph. The inscription on the tomb says simply "Camilla," and then follows the following line of verse: "Soft silken primrose fading timelessly," and the year, 1838. I must say that it took me a moment to identify the source of the line when Nari quoted it to me, and I wonder how many of my readers will be able to place it. For Milton's very early poem "On a Fair Infant Dying of a Cough" is very little known even now. It must have been even less known in the early years of the nineteenth century when the man who mourned Camilla had it inscribed. One can only imagine what kind of a man he must have been to remember an obscure line of Milton in a remote, almost inaccessible area, which he was no doubt engaged in subduing and bringing under the British flag. Nari tells me that no one knows who Camilla was, but it is conjectured that she was a girl born to Captain David Scott, who led the first British troops into the Khasi Hills, and his Khasi mistress, and that her early death left the father inconsolable. Another conjecture is that Camilla was the name Scott had given his beloved. Whatever the truth, I have always found Nari's account of the grave irresistible and often wished that he had guided me to the exact spot, for very few others know where it is. I am touched by the line from Milton, I am touched that it was this poet (on whom I wrote my first book) rather than any other who came as a consolation to a grief-stricken man, and I am touched, too, at the thought that just about the only surviving object from the earliest years of the British presence in the Khasi Hills should be one that bears eloquent testimony to the close relationship between the British and the Khasis.

The area chosen by the British for their new settlement was not totally uninhabited. There were several tiny, scattered villages: Laban, Malki, Jaiaw. and so on. What the British did was to incorporate them into the new city of Shillong; for themselves they chose a small ridge which to this day is called the European Ward and houses the Governor, the ministers, and senior bureaucrats. The villages lost their self-sufficiency and isolation long ago and have become fully part of Shillong. But they still possess certain features which are a throwback to the time when they were small villages, and their inhabitants were suspicious of strangers from neighboring villages. Thus, at the foot of the Malki hill is a sign that announces that you are about to enter Malki village where unruly behavior will not be tolerated and strangers may not move about after dark unless on lawful errands. Each area still elects a *gaon burha* or village elder who is responsible for the cleanliness and general wellbeing of the area under his charge. Since most of these areas, or former villages, are outside the municipal limits of Shillong, much depends upon the keenness and ability of the *gaon burha*. If he orders all inhabitants not to go to work on a particular day but to spend the whole day cleaning the drains, chances are that just about every man, woman and child will obey. It is this reason why Malki, which is heavily populated, is always neat, clean and pleasant.

Perhaps I am being fanciful now, but I sometimes thought that I could sense certain other features that distinguished people of one Shillong locality from another and were thus indicative of the fact that these localities still retain some characteristics of their original village existence. In the past there was little intermingling between the people of different villages; and to this day you will find, I think, that some of the female inhabitants of Jaiaw wear their hair tied tightly in a bun, have rather pinched features and prim mouths, while those in, say, Lumpyngad wear their hair loose, and have rounder faces. These differences may have something to do with the racial variations that evolved in these largely isolated villages over the years; they are, of course, totally unrelated to the various extraneous and accidental differences that have become prominent in recent years, for instance, that a large part of people in Laban are Bengali while those in Happy Valley are Mizos or in Mawkhar Khasis.

The British not only built lovely houses for themselves in the European Ward; they also built a beautiful artificial lake on the edge of the area, called Ward's Lake, and laid fine gardens and what must surely be one of the loveliest golf courses in the country. When Assam came under British rule, Shillong became the capital, and this fact led to tremendous and rapid growth of the town. New areas came up. What had been paddy fields became dwelling areas, only the name of the locality (Dhankheti) serving as a reminder of the past. The area across the river *Khrah* became a shopping area and was appropriately named *Laitumkhrah*, which is the Khasi for "across the Khrah river." A thatched-roof house was built by an Englishman on top of a hill; and when other houses came up on that hill, the hill acquired the name of *La Chaumiere* (since corrupted to *Lachhumere*), which is the French for a thatched house. A big market sprang up which attracted buyers and sellers from a number of surrounding villages. This was the Bara Bazar. A polo ground was built, horse races were organized during the season, and the Army stationed themselves in Happy Valley. In just over thirty or forty years from the time the British founded Shillong, it had developed into a busy and bustling hill station, at once the seat of the Assam government and the holiday resort of the British tea planters of the plains.

The hub of social life was, of course, the club. The original building was burnt down in a fire, and the new cement and concrete structure is not half as beautiful as the one it has replaced. And what days it must have seen! Old timers lament that the club isn't fun any more and that apart from a lot of hard drinking it offers few pleasures. But in the old days there was a library, tennis, cards, balls, and much socializing. People remember the time, thirty or forty years ago, when of an evening you could meet Fakhruddin Ali Ahmed, later to be President of India but then a young lawyer, on the golf course, or Baidya Nath Mukherjee, a famous local politician of yesteryear, at the card table, and a host of other illustrious Indians and Britishers in the lounge of the club. It organized picnics, games, raffles, balls, and charity bazars. Anybody who was anybody belonged to the club, and its active membership extended over all of north-east India. Such, such were the days.

But though the British mixed quite happily with the Indians in the club, they never forgot that Shillong was, to them, a resort and a retreat, apart from being the capital of Assam, and its character could not be preserved until and unless strict checks were applied on the influx of Indians from other areas. They also believed that the Khasis, or for that matter all the tribes of the north-east, should be kept as isolated as possible from other Indians. (The government of independent India, too, has continued to feel this way, especially with regard to the tribals of Arunachal Pradesh). Hence they developed the concept of "restricted areas" and the "inner line." Restricted areas, such as the Khasi Hills, were those where outsiders were not encouraged to settle, while areas within the inner line were out of bounds to anyone who did not have special permission from the government to be there. These concepts, in slightly modified form, still operate in the north-east.

It was in order to keep outside influences out that the British government never allowed Indian nationalists into the Khasi Hills. Shillong had, it is true, local politicians like Baidya Nath Mukherjee and others, but no national leader was allowed to visit the city before Independence. Both Gandhiji and Nehru came to Gauhati but not to Shillong. The British doubtless had reasons for their policy, but one cannot help feeling that this enforced isolation was not, in the long run, good for the Khasis and other tribals. It prevented the development of good transport and communication facilities in the area, and psychologically and otherwise cut the tribals off from the important developments that were taking place in the rest of the country. The result has been that the integration of the hill people of the north-east into the Indian body politic after 1947 has proved to be a painful, bewildering and even traumatic experience for some tribes. Never encouraged by the British to think that their destinies lay with the rest of India, some tribals of the north-east still find it difficult to think of themselves as Indian. The Khasis do not, by and large, suffer from this, as theirs was, after all, only a restricted area, but the Nagas and the Mizos lived within the inner line, and independent India has not yet been able to solve all the problems that this fact has given rise to.

The British policy of protecting tribals by keeping them isolated resulted in another curious fact, this time one of omission. Many visitors to the Khasi Hills are surprised that no tea is grown in the region, though neighboring Assam produces the largest amount in the world, and Darjeeling tea is justly famous everywhere. The reason has nothing to do with the climate or geography of the region. The Khasi Hills, blessed with a cool climate, abundant rainfall, and excellent natural drainage, provide ideal conditions for tea. But though the British knew this, they also knew that the tea industry would require a large-scale induction of laborers from Bihar and Orissa, as happened in Assam. The presence of people who were ethnically and culturally different from the Khasis was not considered desirable by the British, and so no tea plantations were started. In the event, the policy proved to be foolish: the economy of the Khasis was deprived of a most valuable means of growth, while time and social changes are bringing the people of these hills daily in greater contact with other Indians, including a large number of Bihari laborers. It is only recently that the government of Meghalaya has decided to start an experimental tea plantation; and if the results are favorable—and congenial climactic factors lead me to predict that they will be—the economy of the State is going to receive a tremendous shot in the arm and vast new avenues for employment are going to be opened.

The British not only wanted to keep the local people isolated; some even hoped to make Shillong a breeding station for English administrators of India. In an article published in the centenary volume of *The Statesman* Nari Rustomji talks of the curious views of an Englishman on the subject at the beginning of the twentieth century. The worthy gentleman argued that it was proving too expensive to import young men all the way from Great Britain to man posts in the civil and military services. Nor would it do to recruit children born of British parents on the plains of India and brought up there, for the climate of the plains would make them weak, sickly and degenerate. There was, therefore, only one answer. Eugenically selected English couples should be stationed in Shillong and encouraged to have children every year. These children would be brought up and educated in the Khasi Hills, and when they were old enough would be recruited in the Services to rule India. This ingenious plan for turning Shillong into some form of a stud farm came to naught, but it is true that the British who came to Shillong, for short or long periods, bred prolifically. Only, it wasn't British women that they mated with but the local Khasi girls.

Khasi women loved them. If having an English lover was a status symbol, being the mother of a blue eyed, blond haired child was even more so. To this day you will see quite a number of people in Shillong with these characteristics. During the second World War, especially, when a large number of British and American soldiers were stationed in Shillong, I understand that they were much in demand by the local women; and since they, too, were only too happy to oblige, there is a large number of men and women in Shillong today, all in their late thirties and early forties, who obviously had one white parent. I am told that one of the prominent politicians of Shillong belongs to this category.

Even otherwise, relations between the British and the Khasis were cordial and friendly. The British did not practice towards the Khasis the color discrimination which was notoriously prevalent in the plains, and the Khasis, for their part, admired everything to do with the Britisher—his religion, his way of dressing, his language, his customs and his manners. What Tirot Singh did to the early English settlers was forgotten, and English objects and attitudes became a craze. To this day you will find that western fashions, western music, and a general reverence for western things and people is more widespread among the tribal people of the north-east than even in the metropolitan cities of India. If you want to know what the latest fashions in clothes are, or who is the most popular pop singer of the day, or if you wish to find out how fashionable people in the West part their hair, you would do well to go not to Delhi or Bombay but to Mizoram or Shillong. Though the government does not allow foreigners to enter Nagaland, and though those who wish to stay in Shillong for an extended period of time must obtain permission from the government, no foreigner is ever made to feel unwelcome or unwanted. Frances always received brighter smiles from people than I did, and better service and more friendliness, simply because she is an American. Indeed, my own acceptance by the Khasis was made easier because of her, and wherever I went, people were the readier to make me feel welcome if she was with me.

If there is a feeling among the Khasis that with the coming of Independence they fell on rather evil days, there is some justification for it. Shillong remained the capital of Assam, but political power passed to the Assamese who weren't particularly interested in the Khasi Hills. Their concern was for the Brahmaputra Valley, and that is where economic activity was geared up and massive developmental efforts made. The hills remained neglected The Khasis felt they could do little to remedy the situation. Not only did they enjoy little political power in the area where they formed a large majority, they had little economic power too. Such business as there was, was in the hands of the Marwaris. The professions were dominated by the Assamese and Bengali middle class. Doctors, lawyers, teachers, businessmen, tradesmen, civil servants, the police—the Khasis were hopelessly outnumbered in each of these occupations.

The result was exploitation and discontent. Little was done to preserve the forest wealth of the area. Vast tracts of land were denuded of trees. Where the Accountant General's quarters stand in Shillong today was once a beautiful pine forest, which was hacked down to provide accommodation for office workers who were mainly Bengali. The land on the Moti Nagar hill, which, it could be argued, belonged to various Khasi sub-tribes, was sold to non-Khasis at what were even then throw-away prices. The result of this indifference to the local people is still visible today. Few, if any, of the properties in the more desirable areas of Shillong are either owned or occupied by the Khasis, though some of them have the economic means to own expensive property there.

The crunch came when the Assamese decided to impose their language on the Khasis as an official language. Several Khasis speak and understand Assamese because of their close contacts with the people of the Brahmaputra Valley but they thought it highly unfair that they should adopt as an official language one that was not their own. If a foreign language had to be imposed, let it be English, they said, for at least it would be a language in which both they and the Assamese would be at an equal disadvantage. When the ruling Congress party refused to see the point of this demand, the Khasis found that they had no alternative but to seek a State of their own. Williamson Sangma, who was a minister in the Assam government, resigned and formed the All Party Hill Leaders Conference consisting of a number of tribal leaders not only from the Khasi Hills but other areas such as Mizoram as well. Their struggle for Statehood was, as these struggles go, remarkably peaceful. But it was also determined, Success came when Meghalaya was carved out of Assam in 1972 and made a full State of the Indian Union. Indira Gandhi was Prime Minister then, and the Khasis have always felt beholden to her for their State.

The new State was named Meghalaya. It is not a Khasi name, and some Khasis have difficulty pronouncing it, calling it Megh-layer or Megha-layaa. A few express mild resentment from time to time that it was a Bengali who coined this name for their State. But most agree that the name is both beautiful and apt. For Meghalaya is indeed the land of clouds. There are, it is true, some bright and sunny days in the year when from sunrise to sunset you will not see a cloud in the sky. But the usual pattern is that the mornings are sunny, but by ten o'clock clouds form, and even though it may not rain, the sun can be glimpsed only at times during the afternoon. Of course, during the monsoon it can remain overcast for days on end. I used to find that though the daily presence of clouds did not bother me during the summer months, in the winter they would get me down. By the time we had finished breakfast and gone into the garden for a stroll in the pleasant sun, the first clouds would already be forming over the horizon. Half an hour later a cold wind would spread them all over the sky, and then there was no alternative but to go indoors and light a fire. And when this pattern was broken by a clear, windless, cloudless day, I would experience a tremendous soaring of the spirits and go for a long walk through the woods, or work hard and happily in the garden. The air had a sparkle, the trees and the grass looked greener, and spread over the hills was a faint and altogether delightful light blue haze. The clouds can, indeed, be unwelcome at times, but it is only right that they should be evoked every time the name of the State is taken.

Meghalaya consists of three hilly regions named after the tribes that inhabit them. They are the Khasi Hills, with Shillong as its headquarters, the Jaintia Hills with Jowai as headquarters, and the Garo Hills, whose main town is Tura. We never got a chance to go to the Garo Hills. We went to Jowai, which is only an hour's drive from Shillong, on several occasions. But the area we got to know best was the Khasi Hills.

The Khasis are more numerous than the Jaintias and the Garos, with each of whom they have affinities. The Jaintias are, on the whole, more similar to the Khasis than are the Garos. It is not always possible to tell Khasi and Jaintia men apart, though with women it is easier because each community wears a distinctive dress. The languages of the two tribes are also not dissimilar. The Jaintias have, perhaps, been more subjected to Hindu and Bengali influences than the Khasis, but today a majority of people in the Jaintia, as in the Khasi Hills, is Christian. The language of the Garos is totally unlike Khasi or Jaintia. Racially, too, the Garos are supposed to be Tibeto-Burman while the Khasis belong to the Mon-Khmer group. The Garos are shorter than the Khasis, though the Khasis are very short people too; they also tend to have flatter faces. The Garo women wear a colorful *lungi* with a wide border, unlike the Khasi women who wear *jainsems*, which is two pieces of check cloth of equal size, each pinned to a shoulder. Economically, too, the Garos are much more backward than the Khasis.

These differences between the Khasis and the Garos, the two most numerous tribes of Meghalaya, may ultimately cause some political disaffection. Perhaps, too, the Jaintias may one day wish to assert their differences from the Khasis which the latter tend to underplay. But for the time being they are all quite happy to belong to the same State, even though the Khasis are economically stronger than the other two tribes, educationally and professionally more advanced, and have the further advantage that Shillong is the capital of the State and the only real city in the area.

No one knows quite how big Shillong is. The 1971 census placed the population at 93,000. In 1976 the Deputy Commissioner told me that there were about 1,25,000 ration card holders in the city. My own guess would be to place the population above 1,50,000. Shillong has grown tremendously in recent years. Apart from some Bengalis, who crossed over from Bangladesh in 1971 after the war and have stayed on, a large number of Nepalis and quite a few Biharis have come to the city in search of employment. There must be at least four or five thousand Naga students studying in various schools and colleges. And since the late sixties, when trouble in Mizoram began, many Mizo families have settled here. Besides, the presence of the university and various central organizations and Surveys like the Anthropological Survey of India, the Zoological Survey, the Botanical Survey, etc. has caused an influx of professionals from other regions. The full extent of this migration will not be known till 1981 when the next census is taken. But wherever you go for walks in the immediate environs of Shillong, you come across quite unsuspected settlements of Nepalis and others teeming with children. I don't think I shall be wrong if I hazard the guess that Shillong has already crossed the 1,50,000 mark.

The consequences are obvious. The three main markets, Bara Bazar, Police Bazar, and Laitumkhrah, can be as crowded as big markets in Delhi during evening shopping hours. If you stand on the main Gauhati-Shillong road near the club during those hours, you will be amazed at the long and unbroken line of cars, taxis and buses following one another almost bumper to bumper. And the buses, though frequent, can be so crowded that sometimes it is impossible to squeeze into or out of them.

A surprisingly large portion of the population of Meghalaya, in fact, lives in Shillong. Assuming that the total population of the State is just over one million, Shillong would account for twelve to fifteen percent of this population. The irony is that of those who live in Shillong, a large number are not Khasis but what the Khasis call *Dkhars*, or outsiders—Assamese, Bengalis, Nepalis, Biharis, Pathans, Marwaris, etc. Many of them are engaged in small trade and business, while others are professional. Indeed, the Khasis have begun to feel so acutely that they are like a minority in their own capital city that recently a number of laws have been enacted seeking to rectify the situation. According to them, non-Khasis are not allowed to buy immoveable property in certain specified areas of the city except with the specific permission of the District Council. If any non-Khasi is already in possession of property there, he may sell it only to a Khasi buyer or to the State. Only those non-Khasis are exempt from this law who have been living in the State for at least twenty years.

These laws can be justified in that similar provisions exist in a number of tribal areas in India, and they are meant to prevent alienating the tribal from his land through the machinations of manipulators and moneyed persons. The provisions are rather hard on the non-tribals who already own property in Shillong—many of these people are Bengali and Assamese—because if these people should wish to sell their holdings, their market would be restricted and they are not likely to get a fair price. But even this injustice may be condoned as being the inevitable result of securing protection for the tribal community. But Khasis have such a strong fear of being outnumbered in their own State that not very long ago the Meghalaya Legislative Assembly passed a Bill to the effect that no non-Khasi could even settle in Meghalaya, much less buy property, without special permission. The measure was clearly xenophobic; had it become law, it would have had far-reaching and disastrous consequences for the economy of the State besides creating all kinds of unpleasant tensions and antagonisms. But the measure could not become law till the President had given his assent, and that he has rightly refused to do, much to the chagrin of some of the more extreme Khasis.

One feature of all these laws that has never been clear to me is whether a non-Khasi or *Dkhar* is just the plainsman, or whether he can also be a non-Khasi tribal from the north-east, a Mizo or a Naga. Indeed, relations between these different tribes are, at best, rather ambivalent. The All Party Hill Leaders' Conference launched by Williamson Sangma consisted of Nagas and Mizos as well as Khasis. And, from time to time, various leaders of these tribes make statements insisting on the unity of all tribal people. But for all that, tensions do exist between the Khasis, the Mizos and the Nagas, and they have only ben exacerbated by the large-scale influx of Nagas and Mizos into Shillong in recent years. On the whole it would be correct to say that the Khasis are better disposed towards the Nagas than towards the Mizos. The Nagas are respected because they are strong, upright and manly people. They are very popular as tenants because they keep their houses clean and pay the rent on time. When I took a Naga lady, who was a colleague in my department, house-hunting, I was impressed with the readiness with which all the landlords we contacted not only agreed to rent their houses to her, but even offered to reduce the rent simply because she was a Naga. It tends to be otherwise with the Mizos, sometimes if not always. There are occasional clashes between the Khasis and Mizos, and one gets the impression sometimes that relations between these communities are strained.

When a Mizo neighbor very kindly planted a green leafy vegetable in our garden because, he said, it was a favorite food of the Mizos and he wanted us to have some, our *kong* Between was not pleased. Every time we asked her to cook this vegetable, she would either pretend not to understand or else would be so full of hesitations and doubts as to how to set about the task that Frances was at last obliged to cook it herself whenever we wanted to eat it. So one wonders to what extent the laws aimed at protecting the Khasi from exploitation by the non-Khasi are likely to adversely affect the status of the Mizos in the Khasi Hills.

Since the creation of Meghalaya the Khasis are no longer treated as second class citizens in their State, as they were when they were part of Assam. They now occupy top positions not only in politics but also the police, the civil services, academics, and other fields. Moreover, 80 per cent of the jobs at the lower levels in the State government are reserved for its inhabitants. The only field in which they have not made their mark is trade and business, where the majority of big operators continues to be Marwaris. The Khasis express resentment about this from time to time; and, indeed, even non-Khasis tend to be critical of the Marwari hold on business. But the truth is that though the Marwaris may number some unscrupulous people whose only interest is making a fast rupee, there is much for which the north-east should be grateful to the Marwari businessman. For generations he has lived a hard and frugal life in remote and at times inaccessible areas to carry on his business. He has made essential commodities available where none could be found before, He has learnt the local language, and in turn has spread a knowledge of Hindi to non-Hindi speaking areas. He has been, on the whole, well integrated with the local community. Though some Khasis may wish him away, the majority acknowledge however secretly, the good that the Marwari has done to their economy, and if all Marwaris disappeared overnight, the Khasi economy would collapse.

So the Khasis have come into their own at last. This fact needs to be coupled with two or three others. One is that the Khasis are better educated than the average Indian. There are a large number of schools and colleges in Shillong, run by churches as well as by government and private agencies; and, though many of them are not very good, they have helped disseminate education among a wide range of people. Hardly any illiteracy prevails among the young people of Shillong.

Add to this the fact that quite a large number of Khasis are, relatively speaking, well off. There are several without jobs, and many earn very little. But by and large the people have enough to eat, a roof over their heads, clothes to wear, and a little bit of money to spend. Even poor, working class people have at least one decent set of clothes; more or less every Khasi in Shillong has, at one time or the other, taken a taxi. There are hardly any Khasi beggars in Shillong, and one never sees the kind of abject and appalling poverty found in the plains of India.

Further, owing to the establishment of a large number of central organizations in Shillong, there are far more professional and middle class people there than ever before. All these facts, when taken together, mean that Shillong has become a prosperous middle-class town. It is a costly place to live in, but people are able to afford the prices. Most families eat meat at least once a week, can afford a couple of eggs per person every week, often take buses, spend money on clothes, and entertain or wish to be entertained from time to time. You cannot always buy a plane ticket to Calcutta on short notice because the flights are always fully booked, and there are big queues at the bus station and the railway booking counter. Since Meghalaya produces very little of its own, a good many things have to be brought from outside the State. The result is that few vegetables sell at less than three or four rupees a kilo in season, bananas may cost up to 50 paise each, and fish 20 rupees a kilo. Yet people are constantly buying these things. It is a very common sight to see, of an evening, a Bengali clerk returning home from work via the market, dangling on a string from his finger a fish, sometimes only a fish head, which will be his dinner. Cloth shops do a roaring business. Gramophone records and fashion magazines are in demand. Banks have sprung up. Not everybody is rich, by any means, but grinding poverty does not exist.

Yet Shillong continues to think of itself as a small, sleepy little place. By half past seven in the evening all shops are closed. There are hardly any decent eating houses where people may have a reasonable meal at reasonable prices. Except for a few cinemas, which are invariably packed, there is little entertainment. Hardly any plays or concerts are held; when on rare occasions something of the sort does take place, tickets are quickly sold out

The tensions between the big-town aspirations of the people and the small-town mentality of the place produce some unfortunate results, especially for teenagers. Some of them find the lulling, soporific effect of the environment so strong that their intellects simply go to sleep. They become smug; the tribal world sucks them in, and they develop an insular, unquestioning mentality. Others, less willing to give in, become frustrated and rebellious by turns. They feel stifled in a city where, they complain, nothing ever happens. Unable to find creative outlets for their energies and, finding that if you want to expand your mental horizons, Shillong offers little scope, they either long to get out of there for the sake of an education or a job, or else find excitement in sex and drugs. Of course, there are very many talented young men and women who do not fall into any of these categories. But it does remain a fact, I think, that these categories apply to an alarmingly large number of the young.

Recently the youth of Shillong has found another outlet for its pent-up energies and frustrations—politics. In a State where a candidate standing for election to the Assembly is assured of a win if she or he polls 3000 votes, and sometimes just 2500 votes, even five hundred well organized young men and women become a political force to reckon with. It was one such group that herded the newly elected MLAs into the Assembly just after the 1978 election and told them that they would not be allowed to go out until they had agreed on a coalition. The MLAs, as is the wont of most politicians, continued to bicker among themselves, and at one time it looked as if their inability to sink political differences would result in President's rule in Meghalaya for the first time in its history. But though the legislators might not have minded this possibility, the young men and women who were "gherao-ing" them clearly did. They stepped up the pressure, and their elected leaders relented. On the suggestion of the youth a priest was called, who prayed and then decided, by the toss of a coin, which of the two rivals was going to be Chief Minister. The one who lost accepted the post of Deputy Chief Minister.

The coalition did not last long, but that's another story. The important thing is that a few people, some of them not even old enough to vote, had played a crucial role in the political affairs of Meghalaya and brought into being a government which may not have enjoyed the confidence of the bulk of the voters in places outside Shillong. Youth power had come to stay.

That the young are important in Shillong is a very good thing; that they may not always behave responsibly causes the old people to be apprehensive. The answer lies clearly in providing the young with the opportunity to expand their horizons, become less ingrown and insular, and put their power to constructive use. The university has obviously helped in this direction, but much more needs to be done, and neither the government, nor the church, nor the educationists know to how start.

One reason is that all these three groups of people have been affected by the lotus land atmosphere of the place. Take the educationists. I once found myself helping to interview candidates for the post of Principal of one of the leading women's colleges. Almost every candidate expressed him or herself against extra-curricular activities, arguing that such activities detracted students from a pursuit of their studies. And since the concept of study amounts to little more than attending classes from morning till evening and mugging up a textbook just before the exams, it is not surprising that there is a high delinquency rate among the students of that college. Similarly on another occasion I found myself in the office of the Principal of one of the prestigious men's colleges. I had gone to request the use of the college hall for a debate we were organizing. He turned my request down. "I have been a teacher for forty years," he told me, "and it is my considered opinion that things like debates are harmful to students."

The churches are no better. A close friend and classmate of mine at Oxford, John Roche, an Australian, was going to Britain for his sabbatical in 1976, and came to visit us for a week on his way. A devout Catholic, he wanted to attend Sunday Mass, so I took him along to Shillong's Catholic church. Both he and I were appalled and disgusted by the priest's sermon. He said that people would try to mislead his parishioners, often quoting the Bible for this purpose. But they should not listen to anyone except himself, for only he told them what the truth was that they should follow. They should not try to read or learn anything for themselves for they might misunderstand what they read. They should just do what he said.

As for the government, it runs schools and gives scholarships, but there its responsibility to the young ends. It offers no patronage to social services, organizes no art shows or photographic competitions or sports events, and does not do anything to encourage students to travel outside their State. It can't even encourage them to travel within their own State and thus get to know it better, for the simple reason that it has done little to develop roads and transport facilities. The result is that many Khasi students—and not only they—are ignorant not only of all that their State contains, but also of their immediate environs.

Indeed, traveling out of Shillong to other places in the Khasi Hills can be very difficult for those who don't have their own transport. Buses are small, rickety and old; there are also very few of them. You are packed into them tighter than sardines and find yourself clutching on to any handhold, a bar, the back of a seat, the hair of the old woman next to you, every time the bus lurches precariously on sharp turns. Lying at your feet might be a trussed-up pig being taken to the market; occasionally your face is flapped by the bunch of fish that the passenger next to you is holding in his hand. Squawks of chickens alternate with the blaring of the bus horn; there is an oppressive smell compounded of sweat, diesel fumes, pigs' excrement, and the *paan* and *koi* that everyone is chewing around you. If you are a sightseer out to enjoy the beauties of Meghalaya, you may not have much time to enjoy the beauties of Nature since the bus that will take you back to Shillong may already be heard rounding the bend and, if you miss it, you are not likely to get another till the following morning.

With such conditions to contend with, and the government doing little in the matter, it is not surprising that Shillong students know very little of what things are like just twenty or thirty miles from their city. When I went on a university picnic to Mawphlong, just an hour's drive away, I was surprised to find that for at least half the Khasi students on the trip it was their first visit to this place.

Yet Mawphlong is well worth more than one visit. Till a few years ago it used to be famous for its pub, and several tea planters from Assam would travel up regularly for the weekend to sample its specialties. The pub was run by a retired English army officer, Capt. Hunt, who had married a Khasi woman, farmed potatoes during the day, and served cherry brandy and sausages of his own making to appreciative customers in the evening. But with his death the quality of the pub has declined. Its cherry brandy now tastes like cough syrup, sausages are not normally available, and you are served bad food by the sullen survivors of the good Captain's family. The fact is that his heirs have neither an interest in the business nor a vision of what it can be. Sadly, therefore, it has become a mere place for some seedy looking customers to get drunk.

But if, untempted by the dubious charms of this pub, you proceed another mile or so along the road, you will encounter the most spectacular views of rolling downs and, nestling at the bottom of the valley, an enchanted oak forest. The trees are not very old, and the absence of undergrowth suggests that the forest is quite new, though legend has it that it is an ancient sacred grove. Whatever the truth of the matter, there is no doubt that the forest is a glorious experience. Inside, it is deliciously cool and a little dank. Mosses abound; the trees are covered with orchids. Sudden, unsuspected clearings make excellent picnic spots, and as you sit down and unpack your hamper, you will notice all around you a great profusion of lovely wild flowers, while overhead on all sides are thick-leafed rhododendron bushes which burst into scarlet flowers in early May. A visit to the forest will reveal, as few other experiences can, what Keats had in mind when he talked of holy and haunted forest boughs.

There are, in fact, any number of lovely places around Shillong. Shillong Peak, bare and windswept, is the highest point in the Khasi Hills and can afford a view, on a clear day, of a thin silver line to the north which is the Brahmaputra, and, further along in the same direction, the snow-covered Himalayas. Elephant Falls are not far away: here there is only the sound of rushing water, and little sandy banks embowered by trees where lovers may dally without fear of prying eyes. Beadon Falls and Bishop Falls commemorate two Englishmen, and impress the visitor with the deep gorges down which the waters tumble at terrific speed though they seem to hang still in the air, only a roar in the distance indicating that they are, in fact, obeying the law of gravity. There are innumerable other streams, waterfalls and forests, all within a fifteen- or twenty-mile radius of Shillong.

If getting there can be a problem, it is also a blessing. Wherever you go, you can be alone since there are hardly any visitors. And therefore there is hardly any litter, noise or dirt. Just Nature—and you.

That is why it is such a pity that the youth of Shillong know little about these places and are not encouraged by their elders to explore them. If they were, many advantages would accrue. For one thing, conservation both of plant and animal life is an urgent necessity in Meghalaya. The killing of animals is wanton and indiscriminate, as is the felling of trees. It is sad that, in spite of its lovely forests, one hardly comes across any birds in and around Shillong for they have all been killed and eaten. It is a very common sight to see gangs of boys roaming all over the place with catapults trying to kill every bird they see, even if it is only a crow or a sparrow If these boys could be encouraged to love birds and trees rather than destroy them, and if they took to traveling around a bit and getting to know something of their State's flora and fauna, they could become a potent force for the preservation of the environment.

Further, getting to know Nature will result also in in a better acquaintance with the village folk from whom the students of Shillong are getting increasingly alienated, though I must emphasize that this alienation has not, by any means, reached the proportions that exist in other Indian cities of comparable size or culture. The more militant Khasi students are rightly assertive of their Khasi identity, but they know little of Khasi myth, folklore, ways of life, cultural institutions, or religion, apart from what they acquire by the way. Surely they couldn't do better in their search for identity than to get to know the rural people better; and one way of doing this would be for them to go to the countryside more frequently in pursuit of nature studies. More imaginative government, church and educational leaders could make this possible by improving transportation, providing cheap places for overnight stays, relating the teaching of science to local conditions, organizing nature study clubs, holding lectures and exhibitions, and myriad other ways. Unfortunately, nothing along these lines is being done.

There is another way in which the frustrations and ideals of youth can be made to interact creatively with a vital aspect of Shillong's environment. Shillong receives anything between 80" and 120" of rainfall a year. So, other things being equal, there should be no water shortage at any time of the year. Unfortunately, other things are not equal. The water supply system was laid down by the British at the beginning of the twentieth century; and since no attempts were made thereafter to keep pace with the growing population, it has become hopelessly inadequate for the city's needs. There are no water storage facilities, and no attempt at conserving rainwater. Indeed, the Khasis are very prodigal in their use of water. Partly, no doubt, it is because Shillong water is hard, and it takes a lot to get the soap off. Even so, they will use three buckets when others can make do with one, and the idea that it might be a good thing to turn the taps off when not in use appears laughable to them. The result is that at certain times of the year water just gushes out of all the public and private taps and runs to waste, at other times not a drop can be coaxed out of them. Right in front of our house was a public tap, and we noticed hundreds of times the water just running down the drain because the faucet had been left on, or worse, simply stolen. This state of affairs would last for a few weeks, and then one day suddenly there wouldn't be a drop of water, and long lines formed of men, women and unwashed children, each carrying drums, buckets, tin pots, frying pans—anything that could hold enough water for them to be able to brush their teeth with.

The periodic scarcity of water is compounded by another fact that has an ecological origin. Increasingly in the last twenty years or so trees have been cut down in the upper reaches of the hills, and ground cleared for the cultivation of potatoes. As it happens, much of the water supply of Shillong is untreated and unfiltered: several small springs in the hills have been joined through pipes to little metal tanks, from which smaller pipes conduct water to individual homes. So long as the hills were forested, the trees kept the soil in place. But potato cultivation has loosened all this soil, which the streams wash down with them into the metal tanks below. The process becomes highly accelerated whenever there is a heavy shower of rain. From the metal tanks the earth gets into the smaller pipes and clogs them. Thus you often have the spectacle of these metal tanks bursting with too much water which can't flow out because the outlets are choked with mud. Since this phenomenon is, as I have just said, encountered most frequently whenever there is a heavy shower, one of the supreme ironies of living in Shillong is for people to find their kitchen and bathroom taps bone dry because it is pouring outside. It is for this reason that most roofs have little gutters fitted underneath them in such a way that all the rainwater from the roof is guided to a spout under which people place drums. Then every time the taps go dry, you have simply to step out in pouring rain and fill your buckets from the drum. If you slip while carrying the bucket back, it's just one of the hazards you run in your daily quest for water.

The government, in wanting to tackle the problem, has come up with the Greater Shillong Water Supply Scheme, but this scheme has run into snags. For one thing, it envisages the creation of a reservoir over fields and farms which the owners do not wish to part with. In any case the engineering problems involved are such that it will be years before the scheme fructifies, if at all. In the meanwhile, the only thing the government can do, and which it hasn't apparently thought of doing, is to install at all public taps the kind of faucet you find in railway carriage toilets. You have to press the button before water will come and, when the pressure is released, the water also stops. The advantage of this kind of faucet will be that water won't run to waste simply because someone has not bothered to turn the tap off.

But an even more efficacious answer would be to educate people to conserve water. It is here that the youth of Shillong can come in. There is not one locality in the city which does not have some teenage students; and if their educational institutions and church leaders were to encourage them to take an interest in the water problems of their areas, the results would be tremendous. They could talk to their neighbors about the need to conserve water; they could patrol their areas and turn off taps from where water was going to waste; they could repair and replace broken faucets with just a day's training and a few basic tools; and they could help to unclog pipes which had got choked with mud. At present these tasks are meant to be performed by *gaon burhas* and various local committees, but it is generally seen that these individuals and bodies are of little help when taps run dry. Then the only recourse is to find the local plumber and pay him handsomely. If young people were associated with this work, they would not only learn some skills and a sense of responsibility but would also develop an involvement with their local communities. What we lack all over India today is an involvement of the people with the resolution of their problems at the grass roots level. People everywhere are becoming more and more dependent upon the government and ceasing to tackle small but pressing problems on their own. I always felt in Shillong that it was a pity that the talents of the young were not harnessed in the solution of a daily problem that the people of the city face.

As I have pointed out already, there has been a lot of deforestation around Shillong in recent years. Even so, the Khasi Hills are blessed with many forested areas. There are Khasi pines everywhere. One problem with them is that they burn easily, and consequently there are frequent forest fires. In the long run fires caused naturally don't do much damage because vegetation is quick to grow back again, and the land where there has been a fire is made naturally more fertile by the ash. But forest fires can be quite dramatic and need to be put out lest they should spread, rather than being allowed to burn. We were witness to a major fire once.

Frances and I had had a tiff over something very slight. I was in a bad mood, and she was secretly wishing that I would disappear for good, or at least for a good long time. It was then that we noticed thick smoke rising from the hill behind our house one evening. I reported it to the local police station which was only a short distance away. But the police pooh poohed my complaint. They said it was probably just local farmers *jhuming*, or setting the stubble on their land and a few trees around afire to clear and fertilize the area, a practice quite common among the farmers of the hills. The fire looked bigger than such *jhum* as we had seen but the police were quite sure that that

that was what it was; and who was I to dispute the judgement of the police?

But soon the smoke became thicker and more expansive, and occasional flames could be seen. Finally the fire brigade took notice. We heard them lumbering up the hill where we lived. I assumed that they were going to the forest. Instead, two fire trucks drove into our compound. I went out to meet them, and they said they thought our house was on fire. I assured them that our house was perfectly safe, and pointed the fire, very visible by now, out to them. But they did not know the road up into the hills, so I agreed to go along with them as their guide.

So off we drove to the fire, about a mile and a half away, and the firemen forgot all about me and set about trying to put out what was by now quite obviously a major forest fire. I stood there, not at all pleased at the idea of having to walk back home in the dark late at night, when I noticed some more vehicles driving up. One was that of the current Deputy Commissioner of the Khasi Hills, Vinay Kohli, whom we knew, and Hari Jafa, having been alerted, drove up too. So the three of us stood around, talking, watching the firemen do their job, and smoking cigarettes whose unextinguished butts we flicked into the fire. In the meanwhile, Frances was getting very concerned because I had not told her that I was going with the firemen, and I was not home. She had no means of contacting me, and there was no question of her going out to look for me at that hour of the night. So she got progressively more worried, forgot that she had wished me away, and was very relieved when, several hours later after the fire had been brought under control, Vinay dropped me back home in his jeep. All her earlier resentment was forgotten.

The post office played an important part in our lives, as it did in the lives of all people who lived away from home. Letters were our only means of keeping up with our families and friends, and all business with people who lived away from us had to be transacted by mail. There was a big post office in Laitumkhrah, not too far from where we lived, and we were frequent visitors there. The only problem was that we were not the only visitors. There was usually quite a crowd there, so that even a simple affair like buying postage stamps could sometimes take a fair amount of time. A man who had once been a clerk at that facility had sadly lost his mind, and he used to hang around trying to sell bits of paper to all the customers. He was a perfectly harmless person and everyone felt sorry for him and treated him kindly, but he would sometimes cotton on to you and keep pestering you to buy his scraps until you had transacted your business at the window and were finally off. No question but that Frances and I used to find our visits to the Laitumkhrah post office rather trying.

One day, quite by accident, she discovered that there was another smaller post office in Nongthymmai, very close to the university. It occupied a room upstairs in a house that obviously belonged to the lady who ran the office. You could do simple transactions there, but the great advantage was that there were no crowds. If you wanted to buy stamps or aerograms, or send a parcel or a registered letter or a money order, the lady would take care of your needs. She was usually in the room that served as the post office during working hours, but sometimes when she was bored or had decided that no customers were likely to come for another half hour, she would disappear into the recesses of her home. Then, if a customer came, he would call out loudly and she would appear, looking rather annoyed at being thus disturbed, but would take care of the business to be done.

We started patronizing this post office not only because it was so uncluttered but also because we discovered that it was cheaper than the Laitumkhrah one. Either because the weighing machine she had was defective, so that letters and packages always weighed less on it than in Laitumkhrah, or else because the chart that she had for postal rates was out of date, it was always cheaper sending packets and parcels from her little room than from the big post office. And they always reached. I once carried out a test. I had to send a parcel, so I took it down to the Laitumkhrah office and asked the clerk what it would cost. He quoted a price, and then when I brought it to the lady in Nongthymmai she quoted another, lower price. I entrusted my parcel to her care, and sure enough, it reached its destination.

Only in Shillong would two post offices have two different rates for the same service!

No account of Shillong will be complete without a description of one of its most famous institutions, Bara Bazar. Bara Bazar is situated on a small rise at one end of the city. It is big, dirty and colorful, and you can buy just about anything there, from pins to live turtles. The whole area is arranged commodity-wise: you pass along a row of shops selling tin pots, turn into the next alley which has nothing but *paan* and *koi*, then into a third which sells only mutton before entering yet another where all the vegetables available in Shillong are on display, and so on. It is very easy to lose your way in the labyrinthine alleys of Bara Bazar, but so long as you are not looking for any specific shop this is the best way to get a feel of the place. Huge mounds of reddish oranges comfort your sight, to be replaced by wicker baskets of intricate and fantastic design, and these, in turn, yield to great white slabs of lime which the Khasis eat with their *paan*. And then suddenly there are strange looking men exhibiting even stranger wares on a little carpet spread out on the pavement. You can buy tiger's fat, powdered rhino horn, newts' tails, crocodile teeth, and various other objects which, as the local people well know, are indispensable if you wish to cure your rheumatism or improve your sexual prowess. The vendors are always surrounded by knots of curious bystanders, though whether much business is done I never found out. Underfoot it can be quite slippery and squelchy, and you rub shoulders with a quite uncommon variety of people, Khasis, Nagas, Garos, Mizos, Nepalis, Tibetans, Sikhs, Tamils, English, German tourists, Bengalis, Bhutanese, Assamese, Sikkimese, Punjabis. You step aside to allow a man to pass, pipe in his mouth and back bending under the weight of a pig he is carrying, and in the process bump accidentally into a slim Chinese girl hurrying back to work at the hairdresser's after her late morning *chow*. As you stand bargaining for a basket full of oranges, down comes a sharp shower and you walk into a Marwari cloth shop for shelter. No one minds; and it is this sense of the total acceptance of everybody and everything that constitutes the peculiar ambience of Bara Bazar.

Another remarkable feature of the place is that except for the Marwari stores and meat stalls, all other shops are "manned" by women. Men may visit Bara Bazar for business or pleasure, but it is the women who dominate life here. Some are barely in their teens; some others, especially the fruit vendors, are stunning beauties. But most are old, deeply wrinkled, shrewd, with a merry glint in their eyes and a ready, if toothless smile. Their linguistic versatility is fantastic. Khasi speakers all, they are, nevertheless, fully capable of not only bargaining but also joking in Hindi, English, Bengali and Assamese. Whoever said that the tribals of the north-east are resistant to Hindi? Hindi is the second language of Bara Bazar.

Democracy flourishes in Bara Bazar as in few other places in India. There is no high or low, rich or poor. A respected government official with whom you may have been closeted earlier in the day on State business may be seen poking and prodding a fish to test its plumpness. And surely the woman from whom he is buying it was earlier seen sitting primly behind a typewriter in his office earlier in the day? But Bara Bazar has a way of leveling all the hierarchies that societies may create.

On the occasional "Bara Bazar Day", people come to buy, sell, see and be seen from villages as many as fifty miles away. There is much merry making then, and eating and drinking and news swapping, and children scream, matrons scold, and young men and women giggle and smile and feel rather self-conscious in their new clothes, and look everywhere with sparkling eyes. The government runs special buses on Bara Bazar Days, and they run fully laden with people and produce and pigs.

In the rest of the country the big market day comes round regularly once a week. Not so in Shillong. The day of the Bazar is calculated from the time the annual Nongkhrim Dance (about which I shall say more later) will be held by a method of computation that I was never able to understand. The result is that sometimes you can have two Bara Bazar Days in a week, but more often they are eight or nine days apart. You can never look at your calendar and say, "The next Bazar day will fall on Tuesday the 20th." The only way to find out is to ask any Khasi. He or she will always know, though if you ask them how they know, they will say that someone else told them so, and if you ask that somebody else, they will say that they heard about it from yet somebody else.

Unless you have bought so much in Bara Bazar that you have to take a taxi home, you will wish to travel back by bus. Ah, the buses of Shillong! How we loved and hated them. They are unlike any other buses that I have encountered. For one thing, their very presence makes them unique, for I am not aware that there is any other hill station in India which has a regular city bus service. In keeping with the demands of hill roads they are small and low. I am 5 feet 6 inches tall, and were I taller by even an inch, I should not have been able to stand upright in them. They lumber up hills at slow speed, emitting enormous quantities of black, filthy smoke, but when going downhill the drivers just turn the ignition off to conserve fuel, and swerve and careen madly down, blowing their horns all the time and from time to time coming to a very abrupt halt with a jerk that even Delhi bus commuters have not experienced. If you are lucky enough to have a seat, you will find that the seat tilts most awkwardly so that you are constantly sliding off. Moreover, the seats are hard; and since the short Khasis don't need much legroom, it is assumed that no one else does either. The result is that people sit curled or hunched up in all kinds of fantastic and contorted positions, and their faces reflect their agony.

Another remarkable feature of these buses is that they suffer from a kind of sleeping sickness. As soon as they reach a stop, they just go off to sleep, and it may be five or even ten minutes before they are ready to move again. Since there are seven or eight stops between Fire Brigade and Police Bazar, it may take you the best part of an hour to reach one place from the other, though the distance is not much more than three miles. There is no doubt that Shillong buses are bad for anyone who may be in a hurry.

But let me not be too hard on them. You will never have to run for them. Since no bus will start unless another has arrived behind it, you will always find a bus at the stop. When two are standing together there is much competition between the rival conductors for your patronage. One will try to coax you to enter the bus in front because it will leave first, while the other will be equally vociferous in persuading you to enter his because there is more room in it. These conductors are usually boys who are hardly in their teens yet. As soon as their bus pulls to a stop, and sometimes even before that, they jump out and start helping passengers to alight or board. They will not let anyone enter till the last of the alighting passengers is safely out. If an old man wants a helping hand, or a woman needs someone to relieve her of her shopping bag, these boys are most willing to oblige. When the last of the alighting passengers has got off, these boy conductors will ensure that all the boarders get on safely before the bus starts. They will dart half a dozen times between the arms and legs of people already on the bus, asking one person to squeeze further to the left to make room for another, a second not to stick his hand out of the window, a third to move further forward. Only when they are satisfied that everyone is safely inside will they bang the side of the bus and sing out "Ia!" (the Khasi for "let's go!"), and then the driver will start.

Bus fares are high in Shillong. But no tickets are ever asked for, and none given. After the bus starts the boy conductor comes round, and you name your destination and pay. He never suffers from a shortage of change, as his counterparts in Delhi do, and will gladly change a ten or even twenty rupee note. If he should come round again after you have paid, you simply have to inform him of this fact, and that will be enough. These conductors take passengers at their word, and passengers, too, never cheat. I have known passengers who could not pay during the journey because the crowded conditions in the bus made it impossible for the conductor to approach them, to hold the bus up after getting off in order to pay. A tradition exists of complete honesty in this aspect of Shillong's life, and you would have to be a very rank outsider indeed to cheat a boy conductor of his fare.

From time to time you may see from the window of your bus three great slabs of stone standing upright by the wayside, while a fourth rests horizontally at their feet. These stones are a common sight in all parts of the city, and if you go up towards Laitkor Peak, on which the microwave station is located, you will encounter what looks like a veritable Stonehenge. Rather salaciously we called these stones Meghalithic erections. No one is quite sure what they are supposed to represent, or how long they have been around. One common theory is that they mark the sites where important Khasis were cremated in the past. Others say that they mark the places where the ashes of dead leaders were buried. Yet other people will tell you that the three erect stones of varying sizes symbolize the matrilineal Khasi family structure since they are meant to represent the mother, the youngest daughter, and the maternal uncle. Whatever be the truth about them, the fact remains that they are no longer erected now. They also provide convenient resting places for the tired walker; and of an evening, as you drive up to Laitkor, you will find many old people sitting on these stones, smoking, gossiping, playing cards or eating. Pre-history merges with the present without any sense of incongruence.

All my talk of buses and driving may have created the impression that the internal combustion engine provided our chief means of locomotion. This was partly the case, for I used my two-wheel Lambretta scooter quite a lot. It was one of the first scooters in Shillong; and though it served me well, taking Frances and me up steep mountain roads and along hairpin bends and through pouring rain, it also required frequent repairs. Occasionally we took buses and taxis. But our most favored means of locomotion was our own legs. The main roads of Shillong are choked with traffic and polluted with smoke fumes, and therefore offer no joy to the walker. But once you are off the main roads, walking is a great pleasure. The Khasis are inveterate walkers, and will sometimes walk as many as ten or fifteen miles on their way to work. It is good manners, if you encounter someone on a walk, to greet him or her with a polite *Khublei*, which is the Khasi portmanteau word for "good morning," "good bye," "how are you?" and "hello!" And you do sometimes meet interesting people. On one occasion Frances and I were tramping through a very lonely tract of forest when we met a family of north Indians who had clearly lost their way. They asked us for directions; and while we were telling them which way to go, the man suddenly interrupted to ask if I had ever studied in St. John's College, Agra. I was very surprised at this question but answered in the affirmative. Thereupon the man introduced himself. He had been my classmate twenty years ago!

He had been posted to Shillong recently and had already got into the habit of going for long walks. In this respect he was adjusting far better to his new environment than several of my university colleagues who, when it became absolutely necessary for them to walk, would puff and pant up hills and hate every minute of it.

My former classmate and his family were carrying umbrellas. To me this was further proof that they had come to terms with the spirit of the place. For in Shillong it can rain any time. One moment the sun will be shining, and you can find yourself getting drenched the next. All environments call for some adjustment on the part of newcomers; and he who is willing to walk everywhere and carry an umbrella has obviously shaken hands with the *genius loci* of the Khasi Hills.

Chapter 5
THE PEOPLE

*T*HOUGH THE KHASIS HAVE NOT BEEN IGNORED BY anthropologists and historians, their origin and early history are still obscure. However, it is generally acknowledged that they belong to the Mon Khmer group of people, and their language has more affinities with Cambodian or Khmer than with any other. In physical appearance, too, they are not unlike the Cambodians.

How long they have inhabited the hills to which they have given their name is a moot point. Though tribal, they are probably not among the aboriginal inhabitants of the area. One of their legends recounts how it came about that they have no script. On one occasion they had to swim across a river. They were led by their chief, who put the script in his mouth for safekeeping. But a wave came and washed it away, and ever since then they have had no script of their own.

Leaving aside the loss of the script for the time being, their story certainly points to some sort of a migration that seems to have taken place sometime in the past, probably across the Brahmaputra. If this was indeed the case, it would appear that the Khasis must at one time have inhabited the north bank of the river. How they got there in the first place, from where, how long they had lived there, and why they were ultimately forced to migrate, are questions that still await answers.

Till just about a hundred years ago the Khasis practiced their own religion which was a mixture of ethical precepts, ancestor worship, and mythology. The myths were as numerous as they were interesting. According to one that attempted to explain the origin of the world, God created a mountain called the Navel of the World (It is, in fact, a hill just beyond Barapani with a huge crater top, which probably explains the name), and placed seven couples there with strict injunctions to lead a life of virtue. This injunction the couples were unable to obey, with the result that they were driven out into the neighboring hills.

Other myths revolve around the rooster: how the sun was swallowed up by a demon but was ultimately saved by the crowing of a cock, or how there was once a flood but the crowing of a cock caused the waters to recede. The rooster occupies, in fact, an important position in the rituals of the Khasi religion. Cocks are sacrificed on certain occasions; and when someone dies, his corpse is carried for cremation with a rooster suspended from each end of the bier. Figures of roosters are placed, too, on top of monuments that are built to commemorate the dead.

In recent years anthropologists have busied themselves with the forms and rituals of the Khasi religion, but no one has yet attempted to make a full collection of its rich myths. When such a collection becomes available, maybe we shall have a better understanding of their early history.

The first Christian missionaries came to the Khasi Hills a little over a century ago, and their success in converting people was remarkably swift and complete. About 60% or more Khasis in Meghalaya are Christian now; in Shillong the percentage would be higher. The earliest missionaries were the Welsh Presbyterians; the Roman Catholics arrived somewhat later, but they, too, enjoyed great success. In more recent times other brands of Christianity have also proved popular, with the result that in Shillong today you find not only the Welsh Presbyterians and Roman Catholics but also followers of the Church of North India, the Seventh Day Adventists, the Baptists, the Church of God, the Church of Christ, the Pentecostal Church— sometimes there seem to be nearly as many varieties of the Christian religion in Shillong as there are people.

No one has been able to account fully for the success of Christianity among the Khasis. If you ask a Christian priest, he will say, of course, that people began to adhere to this religion because it is true. But people don't give up their original religion that easily. Christianity has been around in India for nearly 2000 years, but there are very few Christians in the country, given its huge population. Why did the Khasis convert so easily? Is it that the old Khasi religion had such a weak hold on people that they embraced Christianity without much fuss and bother? This would seem unlikely, especially in view of the fact that a small minority of Khasis still clings tenaciously to the old religion. Is it, then, that the Khasis so loved the Englishman (almost all missionaries were British) that they were willing to adopt his religion simply because it was his? This is probably a sounder theory. But it must be added that if the Khasis loved the British, the British too did everything in their power to earn and keep this love. They brought schools and hospitals where none had existed before. They learnt the language of the people and enabled it to develop by translating the Bible into it. And they went into the remotest villages and made them their home. A common joke in the Khasi Hills goes that when, after Independence, the government decided to build roads to connect Shillong to far-flung villages, the road builders found, on reaching these villages, that each of them already had a church and a missionary in residence. Even today such development as you see in the villages is more due to the single-handed efforts of a missionary than to five-year plans and governmental effort.

A curious feature of the Christianity of the Khasis is that though they have abandoned their old religion, they have not abandoned either their tribal ways or the superstitions and some practices of that religion. One or two instances should suffice. There was once a man who left his wife and started living with another woman. A priest went to remonstrate. The man saw him coming and shouted, "Remember, Padre, though I am a Christian, I am a Khasi first!" Thereafter the church left him alone.

Again, many Khasis, Christian and otherwise, believe in U Thlen. U Thlen is supposed to be an evil spirit who comes in the form of a black cat or a small worm-like snake. In the latter shape he is kept locked up in a box. But every once in a while he assumes the form of a giant snake, and then nothing will propitiate him but a child's blood. On these occasions the devotees of U Thlen keep a lookout for children. If they can kidnap and later sacrifice a child, nothing like it. But if no kidnapping is possible, the next best thing is to take a small clipping from a child's clothes and present that to U Thlen instead. If the sacrifice is accepted, the child from whose clothes the clipping was made will soon sicken and die. In return, the appeased Thlen grants great riches to his devotees.

The superstition is laughable, but what is not is that so many Khasis believe it. Everyone claims to know someone who has become tremendously rich through worshipping U Thlen. Everyone can tell you horror stories of murders and child sacrifices that have occurred. People are afraid to go out alone after dark;

on buses they take special care to see that no one snips
a small piece of material off their garments. If you
argue that there is no place for U Thlen in Christian
belief, people will agree—and go on believing.

Indeed, the Khasi dedication to Christianity is an
important feature of their lives and absorbs a great deal
of their attention. When people sing spontaneously out
of happiness, chances are that it is a Christian hymn
that will come to their lips. Most men and women
attend church every Sunday; some go to two or three
services. Much of the social life of people is centered
round their church: it is there that they meet friends,
it is under its aegis that they go on picnics.

There is no doubt, too, that the coming of
Christianity has helped the Khasis in many ways.
Thanks to missionaries they enjoy the blessings of
education and modern medicine. Above all, their
religion has given them a sense of dignity in themselves
as human beings and a sense of worth. If the average
Khasi considers himself or herself to be a civilized
human being and holds his or her head high, thanks
must go largely to the Christian church.

But in some other ways Christianity has proved to
be a mixed blessing. For one thing, it has alienated
the Khasis to an extent from their history, myths and
customs. Worse, it has alienated many of them from
the rest of the country. It has made them suspicious
of, and sneering towards, the plains Indians who,
many think, worship strange and terrible gods in

savage and uncouth ways. And the more they feel themselves to be unlike other Indians, the more they tend to identify with the West. Many Khasis take pride in not knowing Hindi and being ignorant of Indian history. They also take pride in seeing western films, dressing in western clothes, and listening to western music. Unlike other Indian Christians, the Khasis have failed to indigenize their Christianity, and their sense of not being at ease when they mingle with other Indians, or visit other parts of India, may be attributed to some extent to this failure.

For its part, the church has not always encouraged the indigenization of the religion it preaches. This fact is, perhaps, not strongly marked in Meghalaya; but it is sometimes said that in Nagaland and Mizoram a connection existed in the past between missionary activity and insurgency. The view, held mostly by people aligned with the Government of India, is that insurgents have been encouraged by foreign missionaries with advice, money and arms, in addition to an insistence that their religion has set them apart from other Indians.

The Protestant form of Christianity that came to the Khasi Hills was of the fundamentalist and evangelical kind. There was much emphasis on prayer and singing and salvation, and little on an intelligent confronting of doubts or on study and scholarship. The result was that if it attracted the musical Khasis with its hymns, it also made an already insular people more insular. Though it brought education, the purpose of education was never seen as one of encouraging people to ask questions. Rather, they were encouraged to believe in the literal truth of the Bible and to regard all doubt as devil-born. The Khasis have suffered as a result of these attitudes. They may pray all the time, but they have not necessarily learned to understand the recesses of their own hearts. Self-introspection is rare; a naive and superficial attitude, received wholesale from preachers and adopted unquestioningly, is more generally in evidence. Everybody reads and reveres Billy Graham, but even among the educated Khasis it would be a rare individual who has heard of St Augustine or Dietrich Bonhoeffer.

The Roman Catholic church has been, if anything, even more anti-intellectual than its Protestant counterparts. The Protestant churches at least encourage Bible reading and study individually and in small groups. The Catholic church, to the best of my knowledge, does not do that. I have already mentioned in a previous chapter how appalled my Australian friend and I were by the sermon we heard in the Catholic church in Shillong advising the congregation to refuse to listen to people who held a different faith lest their own should be weakened by the arguments and questions of others.

As an English teacher I found frustrating what struck me as a non-intellectual attitude of a number of my students. They found it frightening to question any kind of authority. They took other people's writing at face value. They liked Spenser simply because he was a Christian poet, though my Catholic students never could get over his anti-Catholicism. Since T.S. Eliot became a Christian in later life, they assumed that his later poetry was bound to be superior to the earlier. Teaching Milton posed problems because though they spotted all the references to the New Testament, they were completely bewildered by the more numerous allusions to the Old. Indeed, I sometimes found myself griping at all the churches for having turned some of my students into smug, unthinking and unimaginative people, and saying that if religion had saved souls, it had also caused them to lose the culture of the mind.

The Christianity that came to the Khasi Hills has never emphasized the fact that it has released in people in other lands one of the most fertile springs of creativity. The names of Bach, Michelangelo, Fra Angelico mean little to Khasis. Music for them tends to be the hymns they sing in church and the Rolling Stones and other pop music they hear out of it. As for the painting, sculpture, or architecture that Christianity has inspired, the church has been quite content to leave its Khasi followers in darkness and ignorance. No, the missionary among the Khasis has not proved to be an unmixed blessing.

However, as I said earlier, the translation of the Bible into Khasi has helped to develop that language and make it more sophisticated. The Khasis take great pride in their language and will warm to anyone who makes an attempt to learn it. People who plan to live in the Khasi Hills for some time would do well to pick up at least a rudimentary knowledge. Indeed, one reason why Khasis often look askance at the Bengalis is because the latter have made no attempt to learn it though they have lived there for years.

Basically, Khasi is not a difficult language, though like any other it has nuances and idioms that are not easily mastered. To one hearing it spoken for the first time, it sounds rather like ducks clacking. The k sound predominates. Once you begin to study it, however, the sounds cease to surprise or annoy. You quickly discover the two most basic facts about the language. First, verbs are not conjugated. Second, articles can be masculine or feminine (u or ka) with the latter predominating, and they are used far more frequently than in English, so that a sentence, translated word for word into English, might go something like this: "The cow that is the black eats the grass that is the green." I soon learned these characteristics of Khasi because my students tended to carry them over into their written and spoken English. Even my better students found it difficult to say "I don't" but "he doesn't" - or "I go" but "it goes." For them, "he don't" and "it go" seemed more natural and logical. Similarly, many students would sprinkle the definite article liberally throughout their sentences, so that whereas in Delhi I had to use my red pencil to insert them into students' sentences, in

Shillong I found myself using the same pencil to excise them ruthlessly.

Tenses in Khasi are simple too. There is the simple present, the simple past, and the simple future. That's all. This makes the language easy for the learner but causes all kinds of difficulties to the native speaker who wishes to acquire another language.

Whereas the above features would make Khasi appear to be a simple and basic language without subtle or complex distinctions, it has other features to show that in its own way the Khasi mind can be as complex as any other. In English we indicate space and distance by saying *here* and *there*. These categories appear to the Khasi to suffer from a lack of proper discrimination. Where exactly is here or there? he or she would ask. I can say, for instance, that my wife is sitting there, a bird is sitting on that tree there, a man is standing down there, there is the sun shining in the sky. In each case the word *there* indicates a lesser or greater distance from the speaker. Khasi makes allowances for this. Moreover, it also has means of indicating whether the speaker is on the same level as the object being described, or above or below it. Thus, depending on the context, the simple word *there* may be translated as *hangtai*, *hangte*, *hangtha*, *hangthei*, etc.

One of the most commendable things that NEHU did in the years we were there was to start a Khasi class for non-Khasis. Frances and I promptly enrolled ourselves. If we did not learn much, the fault was partly our own: we seldom did our homework. But we found, too, that no pedagogical tools exist for teaching the Khasi language. There aren't even basic grammar and exercise books, not to mention more sophisticated tools like audio-visual aids. The teachers had to invent lessons and draw up lists of simple words for us to learn as they went on. And since, for all their enthusiasm, they were quite ignorant of language teaching methods, their attempts were haphazard and unscientific at the best of times. Shillong now houses branches of the Central Institute of English and Foreign Languages (CIEFL) and the Central Institute of Hindi. Both these Institutes have impressive facilities for developing language learning aids and vast experience in training language teachers. If some sort of a program could be drawn up whereby Khasi language teachers would be enabled to avail themselves of the expertise of these Institutes, a very useful service would have been performed.

In the meanwhile, our two teachers managed as best as they could. One was a Khasi, the other a Bengali who had lived in Shillong for many years and spoke the language perfectly. Their different approaches provided a fascinating contrast. The Khasi gentleman never tired of emphasizing the difference between his language and Sanskrit-based languages. Often his sentences would start: "In your language you people say..."and end, "...but in Khasi we say. ..." The Bengali teacher, on the other hand, lost no opportunity to point out similarities between Hindi or Bengali and Khasi. Through what appeared at times to be very dubious etymology, he would argue that the Khasi word for teacher (*nonghikai*) was nothing other than a corruption of the Hindi *shikshak*, and so on. He took special pleasure in pointing out, too, that a very large number of Khasi words were really borrowed from Hindi: *dawai, dukan, mez* (for table). In short, while the native Khasi teacher tried to make out a case for radical differences between his language and those of the rest of India, the Bengali teacher was at pains to suggest that Khasi could be regarded as being very close to Hindi or Bengali because it was, to a great extent, derived from them.

Though these contrasting attitudes were fascinating, both our teachers were, unfortunately, arguing in the dark and allowing their political and cultural proclivities to color their views. For the fact is that not enough is known about Khasi to warrant one or the other view. Here is a magnificent research area for linguists. The philology and etymology of the language have yet to be determined, reliable dictionaries prepared, and its grammar, syntax and structures studied. In the absence of such work most statements about the language would be conjectural , and our knowledge of the history and institutions of the Khasis would remain incomplete. This being so, I have always thought it a pity that the university has not considered it necessary to set up a department of Linguistics to carry out the much-needed research. Such a department could interact fruitfully with the departments of anthropology and history and make a real contribution to our knowledge as well as to more practical problems such as national integration and language teaching.

A further task that linguistic researchers may set for themselves would be to study the regional variations of Khasi. It is generally agreed that the best form of the language is that spoken in Cherrapunji. But because Khasi villages have, until recently, been comparatively isolated, several regional varieties of the language have developed in different areas. If you travel just ten miles out of Shillong you will come across words and forms that may sound strange; if you go to Nongstoin in the West Khasi Hills, over fifty miles from Shillong, it would seem as though a different language is being spoken. With increased transport facilities and growing communication these linguistic varieties may disappear and Khasi may become standardized; in the meanwhile, they cry out for the attention of the serious scholar.

We were naturally curious to know something about the literature of Khasi. We found that though oral literature exists, it is largely unrecorded and unstudied. Certainly, we were not able to experience any. Written literature is just about a hundred years old. There is a reason for this. Till the British came, the Khasis knew no script, and it was the British who made writing in Khasi possible by teaching people the Roman script. (In fact, all tribal languages of the north-east use the Roman script). Since then, Khasi has produced a few essayists and short story writers whose work is not available in translation. However, the poems of U Soso Tham, the most famous poet in the Khasi language, have recently been translated into English. The translations are not good, but they suggest that Soso Tham wrote much on Nature and man's integration with it and sang the glories of his people. He had studied English and, every once in a while, I would meet a budding Khasi scholar who wished to research the influence of Keats or Shelley or Byron or Shakespeare or Milton on Soso Tham's poetry. I began to feel after a while that he must have been a remarkable poet indeed to have drawn from such a heterogeneity of sources. When a monument was erected to commemorate Shillong's centenary, Nari Rustomji, who was one of the chief speakers, recited some lines from the poet in a most rhetorical and impressive fashion. He then went on to translate them: "Trees have been known to move, and stones to speak!" It would seem from this that one way in which Soso Tham was influenced by Shakespeare was that he simply translated bits of the Bard and incorporated these passages into his own poetry. But I must say that, not having read U Soso Tham in the original or devoted more than a very casual and passing attention to the translation of his works, I am not at all competent to comment on his achievement.

Ultimately it is not writers who have helped in the development of the Khasi language but the translation of the Bible into it. If I knew more about the language, I should be able to speak on this subject with greater authority. But it seems to me that the translators must have faced a very difficult task; and, in the process of performing it, they created several new structures and usages which have now passed into common currency. However, since it was the Authorized Version that was translated, it was inevitable that the Khasi translation should have been somewhat high-flown and literary. I understand that some people are beginning to find the Khasi Bible inadequate for this reason; and since they feel, too, that the language has acquired greater suppleness and flexibility in the intervening years, a new, more colloquial translation is in order. When this translation appears, it would be interesting to see what effect it has on the language and its creative use by writers.

Since our aim in learning Khasi was to pick up enough simple, in fact basic, language to be able to carry on elementary conversations, our teachers decided to give us some practice in spoken Khasi. We were taught a dialogue that went somewhat like follows:

Customer: Good morning.

Shopkeeper: Good morning.

Customer: Those pineapples look good. Are they
             sweet?

Shopkeeper: Yes, very sweet.

Customer: How much are they?

Shopkeeper: They are two rupees each.

Customer: That is too much. Will you sell them
             for one rupee each?

Shopkeeper: Certainly Sir.

Customer: I will take three.

We were thrilled to find that getting shopkeepers to lower prices was so easy in Khasi. Armed with our notebooks Frances and I went to the local fruit market after our class.

"Good morning," I said to the girl and smiled brightly.

"Good morning," she replied.

We were delighted to note that the dialogue we had learnt in class was actually spoken in the streets of Shillong.

"Those pineapples look very sweet. How much are they?"

"Five rupees each," the girl replied without batting an eyelid.

Here was a setback. Could our teachers be so ignorant about the market conditions of Shillong? But we didn't lose heart.

"That's too much. Will you sell them for one rupee each?"

The girl replied with a torrent of Khasi speech for which our teachers had not prepared us. All I could make out was that what she said didn't sound at all like the Khasi equivalent of "Certainly Sir." I must have looked blank, for she proceeded to give an English translation of her Khasi speech, What she was asking us, in effect, was whether we thought she was mad.

Embarrassed, and quite, quite out of our depth as far as Khasi was concerned, we beat a retreat. No, I can't say that our attempts to learn the language produced any practical results.

This particular shopgirl was called Berate. Let this not surprise anyone. Khasi names are among the most unusual that we have ever encountered. While many of them are perfectly ordinary, any word or group of words in the English language can serve as a proper name for Khasis. The university rolls were full of Augustborn Sons and Thank Yous and Thriftys. A friend of ours knew three sisters, the eldest of whom was Rivulet, and the middle one Streamlet. The fond mother departed somewhat from reason, if not from rhyme, by calling the youngest Coverlet. It became quite a hobby of ours to collect unusual names. The Vice Chancellor's wife contributed a gem to our collection by telling us about her chauffeur who was named Electricity and whose wife was Terylene. They had three children whom the father, keeping his profession in mind, named First

Gear, Second Gear and Third Gear. Then he took to family planning. Therefore, when a fourth child arrived quite unexpectedly, he promptly named him Accident. I have always thought it a mercy that for this name he changed gears, otherwise the boy might well have had to go through life with the name of Neutral. Another little gem came to us from our friends the Jafas. They told us of a girl who was christened Fair Price Shop Lyngdoh. Finding, when she grew up, that her name attracted unwelcome male attention, she filed an affidavit in court seeking to change her name to Controlled Rate.

One of the most remarkable things about Khasi society is that it is matrilineal. This means that property passes to the youngest daughter of the family, who manages it with the advice of her maternal uncle. Women do not change their names after marriage, and the children take the mother's surname rather than the father's. When a wedding takes place, it is not the girl who leaves her father's house to live with her husband, but rather the husband who leaves his home to live with his wife. If the wife doesn't like her husband, she can simply put his shoes outside the door. This means that the husband has to pack up and leave; as for the wife, the house, the property and the children are hers, and she will stay. When forms have to be filled for admission to schools, jobs, etc., it is not unnatural to find a column asking for the mother's name, when in the rest of the country one has to mention the father's.

The matrilineal system has produced some interesting repercussions in society. For one thing, women are not looked down upon or treated as inferior or second-rate citizens. After all, it is they who inherit property and pass on the family name to children. Therefore women are encouraged to go in for education, take up jobs, and value their importance in the community. On the other hand, boys are sometimes ignored or given second-class treatment. Recently some young men in Cherrapunji found that they were being deprived of their rights to such an extent that they had to start a Men's Liberation Movement! It was our experience that more girls went in for higher education than boys, who not infrequently lagged behind in their studies, and sometimes dropped out of school altogether. A friend of ours who taught school corroborated our experience. He had observed, he said, that till they entered puberty, Khasi boys were pretty much on a par with girls. Thereafter, the girls forged ahead while many of the boys became sullen, dispirited, and lackluster. Our friend concluded that this development coincided with the boys' realization that in some respects their position was no better than that of drones in their society.

As a result of the matrilineal system Khasi girls possess greater dignity, freedom, openness and a greater sense of equality than their other Indian sisters. Visitors to Shillong are often struck by the natural and unaffected behavior of girls, and sometimes they think that because Khasi girls are always willing to talk to you freely and look you straight in the eye, they must have loose sexual morals. Nothing could be less true, though there is no denying that they are not as conservative or straitlaced, as timid or as oppressed, as other Indian girls. Nor are they squeamish about sex. They will go to bed with a man if they want to; if they don't, they won't. That's all there is to it. They are not promiscuous or "loose." They simply take sex much more casually than plains people. Sometimes they just start living with the man of their choice; and when this happens, the relationship is seen as a common law marriage even though it may never have taken place in a church.

Illegitimacy is neither a stigma nor a problem in Khasi society. Not that Khasi girls welcome children out of wedlock. But if one comes, the girl's parents and relatives don't kick up a great fuss. The child enjoys the love of his mother and takes on the mother's last name. The point about illegitimacy is that the child does not know who the father is and cannot assume the father's name or inherit his property. But in a society where the father is not very important and gives neither his name nor his property, which in any case belong to the woman, to his child, illegitimacy ceases to be an issue altogether. This is not the least of the good points of a matrilineal system. We knew any number of young women in our locality who had had children, though they were unmarried. This fact was never held against them, nor were the children made to feel unwanted in any way.

The attitude of the church towards the sexual *mores* of the Khasis is ambiguous. Though it preaches chastity and abstinence from pre-marital sex, and though it may excommunicate a woman who has conceived out of wedlock, it tends, by and large, not to take too harsh a view of the matter. For one thing, a girl excommunicated by one church can always go and join another. She can also return to her original church after a sufficient time has been allowed to pass. The consequence is that people are always flitting out of and back into churches, churches keep frowning on sexual laxity, and girls keep getting pregnant in and out of wedlock. No one really minds or gets terribly upset.

Up to a certain age, Khasi girls tend to stick together. It is a very common sight to see two or three of them walking down the street, arms linked, trying to keep warm in one shawl shared equally by each. But when they start going out with boys it is not unusual to find that they show a preference for non-Khasi boys. For the girls are progressive, intelligent, and ambitious, while a good many, though by no means all, Khasi boys tend to be rather dull, sullen, reckless, or unstable. It is extraordinary that while Khasi boys hardly ever marry non-Khasi girls ("Which girl will marry them?" a rather fiery Mizo girl once remarked), a number of Khasi girls end up marrying non-Khasi men. This must be galling to Khasi manhood, and perhaps explains why in recent years there have been a number of incidents where non-Khasi men were beaten up by Khasi youths because they were seen in the streets with Khasi girls. Indeed, some social and tribal pressure is being brought to bear upon Khasi girls to choose boyfriends from among members of their own community. While these tactics may have succeeded in a few cases, many girls rightly resent this attempt to run their lives and will not be cowed down. They have always enjoyed a preeminent place in their society. Except for politics, which is largely a male preserve, there is no walk of life where they haven't made a mark. Therefore they are unlikely to be brow-beaten by men or allow chauvinistic appeals to sway them.

There is another reason why I am all in favor of marriages between Khasi women and non-Khasi men. Since the children of such marriages are Khasi, this seems to me to be an excellent way of bringing fresh blood into the Khasi tribe. Indeed, such marriages may be rendered inevitable by time itself, for the Khasis are such a small community that in only a short time from now, unless they marry outside the tribe, they will be forced to marry blood relations, which will not be desirable at all. It has always been my contention that the marriage of Khasi women with non-Khasi men is a paradigm of the best features in Khasi society, viz. its ability to assimilate a variety of external influences while remaining true to itself.

If Khasi men do not see the matter from quite the same point of view, it is not merely because they feel that their manhood is at stake. Their objections are to be viewed as part of a larger problem of a tribal society undergoing painful but inevitable changes towards modernization. All Khasis want to enjoy the political and economic benefits that lure people all over the world. They want to be able to control their own destiny and enjoy the advantages of modern technology. But to be able to have the good things of life they have to end their isolation and participate more fully in national life. The inevitable consequence of this will be that they will find themselves in competition with people from other parts of the country; and since the others have more experience of this kind of competition, the Khasis are likely to lose out in the short run. This they find unacceptable. They would like to modernize, but without paying too high a price; they want fish but don't want to get their feet unduly wet. Hence, they want to end their isolation from the rest of the country on their terms: they want modernization but no competition, greater prosperity but no more outsiders in their State; they want to compete for all-India jobs, but they also want special reservations and privileges for the Scheduled Tribes to continue. They do not want special reservations for them to be taken away.

Whether such a compromise is possible, whether it will be possible for the Khasis to become modern and yet retain their old tribal ways and sheltered life, only time will tell. In the meanwhile, the tribal system is feeling the burden of modernization. Incidents such as the beatings administered to non-Khasis for going out with Khasi women, or the recent sad and bloody riots against "outsiders" in Shillong when the Army had to be called out, may be seen as the painful process of disintegration that has begun to afflict the tribal pattern of life.

There can be no doubt at all that at its best a tribal society is a happy and harmonious society. The individual feels a sense of total integration with the tribe; or rather, the individual is not even aware of his own individuality. That quality has been subsumed in the larger entity of the tribe, and he is happy that this is so. He grows up protected by the tribe. If he has any needs, the whole tribe comes to his help, just as he will help others most willingly when the need arises. A tribal society is, in fact, a perfect example of the way one can live for all, and all for one. Economic disparities among tribals are minimal. There is no sense of high or low. Everyone knows everyone else; everyone follows the same customs, shares the same values, and partakes in all the joys and sorrows of the community.

It is an idyllic, if limited, existence, and is clearly incompatible with industrialization, technology, and modern forms of government. The gradual modernization of the Khasi Hills has inevitably resulted in a loosening of tribal ties and values. People are becoming more aware of themselves as individuals. They are more willing to disregard tribal values and loyalties, and the community is finding it increasingly hard to make its will prevail. Economic disparities are beginning to grow, so that today one can speak of the rich Khasi and the poor. Further, a class system has come into being. Though not by any means as pernicious or repressive as the Hindu caste system, of which the tribal knows nothing, it is resulting in exploitation. The middle class, consisting of professionals engaged in education, law, medicine, the civil service, and business, sees its interests as being more closely allied to those of a comparable class of outsiders. Working-class urbanites, students, clerks the petty bourgeoisie, etc., on the other hand, feel threatened by the encroachment of foreign values. They are the conservatives who are fighting to keep "outsiders" and their ideas out. They claim that the reason they are against outsiders is that they don't want a Tripura-like situation where non-Tripurans outnumber the locals. Already, it is being pointed out, Khasis are in danger of being reduced to a minority in Shillong. There is some force in this argument; but I will still maintain that the real reason for their resentment of outsiders is not the fear of being swamped, but has to be sought in the birth pangs of modernism and the gradual emergence of class distinctions.

The middle class, because of its superior economic power and greater education, is able to enjoy the benefits that the Indian government makes available to tribals. The result is that those who already have enough are enabled to have more, thanks to their status as members of Scheduled Tribes, whereas the really poor tribal, for whom these benefits are meant in the first place, gets left out in the cold altogether, or at best can enjoy only what the powerful middle class of his own community is willing to dole out to him. I saw poignant examples of this in NEHU quite often. It is obligatory for each university class to have at least 40% tribals from the north-east. In actual fact, the proportion tended to be much higher. Excellent, you will say, this is just how things should be. But who were the tribal students who constituted 60% or 70% of each class? They were the sons and daughters of government officials, politicians, ministers, ambassadors church leaders, teachers, and owners of land and other property. These were the people who got admission, scholarships and other concessions. The poor farmer, the constable on the beat, the domestic servant, the man without property—they could hardly hope for a university education for their children.

Of course Khasi society is not at all as exploitative or as rigid in its class distinctions as the rest of Indian society; tribal values have not lost all potency. There *were* at the university students from the poorer classes, and sometimes they did well. I was always happy to have such students in my tutorial groups. But by and large the pattern was as I have described it.

I would not like to give the impression that the average Khasi is particularly aware of class and other distinctions, or feels awed or bewildered by them, or carries a sense of resentment against outsiders all the time. Far from it. For the most part, he or she is a very relaxed individual whose great desire is to enjoy life as it comes. Three items that are very high up in his/her list of things to be enjoyed are food, drink, and music.

The Khasi has not contributed to the culinary arts of India. For the most part he eats simply, rice forming the staple of his diet. He does not show a marked preference for boiled food, as the other hill tribes of the north-east do, or for hot, spicy food, as the south Indians do, or for roast or baked or exotically spiced food. Just ordinary, workaday curries are enough for him. He is not a great consumer of milk or milk products (indeed, most of the dairy business in the Khasi Hills is in non-Khasi hands), and will often drink black tea because he doesn't like the taste of milk. Nor do sweets figure prominently in the Khasi diet, though he will willingly eat Bengali sweets when he can get them. He knows little of puddings and cakes. What he does enjoy are two items for which non-Khasi show no partiality at all. One is a particularly strong-smelling *chutney* made out of radish and garnered liberally with dried fish. The other is *jaddoh*, or rice cooked in blood, usually pig's blood. Other Khasi delicacies tend to be of the same variety.

Though he may be forced by economic circumstances to be a vegetarian, the Khasi loves meat. The kind most often preferred is pork. Villagers rear pigs in order to sell them at exorbitant prices at Christmas time, and no wedding feast is complete unless there is at least one pork dish. (It is the Khasi fondness for pork, by the way, which explains why so many of them suffer from worms). But other kinds of meat will do just as well—mutton, chicken, fish, and beef. Of them, beef is the cheapest, and therefore eaten in great quantities.

A word must be said about beef in the Khasi Hills. The hills of the north-east are now probably one of the few places in India where cow slaughter is permitted and the Khasis, as also the other hill tribals, are very jealous in guarding their freedom to eat beef. The recent agitation of Acharya Vinoba Bhave to ban cow slaughter upset them greatly, and further alienated some of them from the mainstream of Indian life. Therefore, they were very relieved to find that Acharya Bhave was agitating to have cow slaughter banned only in Bengal and Kerala. This was one occasion when the Khasis were actually grateful that the leaders and saints of India paid little attention to their existence.

Though the presence of a cattle breeding farm in Upper Shillong run with the help of the Danish government has done something to improve the number and breed of cows in Meghalaya, the State does not have enough cows for beef. The bulk of those slaughtered comes from the plains. Any time you drive down to Gauhati you will encounter herds of the most sick and pathetic looking animals being taken to the hills for eventual slaughter. Their owners are quite often Nepalis and Biharis who themselves are opposed to beef eating but not adverse to selling their cattle to be eaten. The sight of these really miserable looking cows is enough to put you off meat eating for good.

Pork, beef, fish, chicken, mutton—lots of other people eat them also. But the Khasis don't stop here. Shortly after we moved into Arden, we found ourselves being plagued by rather ugly-looking green spiders. The trees and bushes were full of their webs, and as you walked underneath, there was always the concern that one of them would drop down on you. Imagine our surprised pleasure, therefore, when one afternoon a horde of children from the neighborhood arrived in our garden armed with brooms, sticks and twigs and began systematically to sweep all the cobwebs away. Here, we said, in tones of admiration, was the tribal spirit at its best. Our neighbors had found out that we were being plagued by spiders, and they had sent their children to rid us of this nuisance. We persisted in this belief till we were informed that our neighbors weren't as altruistic as we had thought . Their children were merely collecting their dinner.

I say "dinner" advisedly, for few Khasis eat lunch. Many will do with two meals a day: early in the morning, and then again at night. During the day they assuage pangs of hunger by consuming innumerable cups of tea and eating light snacks or *jingbam*, usually fried rice cakes and stale and unappetizing looking pastries.

Khasis also love to drink. There are, of course, exceptions. The church disapproves of this habit, and a temperance movement exists in the State. Recently, too, the government has declared itself in favor of eventual prohibition and, as a first step in that direction, no new liquor shops are allowed to open, and existing ones have to observe dry days. This does not prevent a good deal of drinking going on all the time. Unfortunately, Khasis can't always hold their liquor well, and one comes across several instances of drunkenness. When the Khasi gets drunk, he gets classically drunk. He behaves exactly as a bad actor who is playing the role of a drunk. He will stagger blindly from one end of the street to the other. He will speak in an incoherent and theatrical way. He will become obstreperous and get into fights. He will stand at his doorstep and hurl abuse at the whole world at the top of his voice. He will sing loudly, urinate in his pants, and go off to sleep in the gutter, oblivious to the world. The newcomer to Shillong gets inured to these sights soon enough and takes extra precautions while driving at night lest he should knock down a drunken man who lurches suddenly across his path.

All India-made "foreign" liquors—beer, whisky, rum, gin—are popular with the Khasis. They also produce a sweet rice beer, as do many other tribals. But what they prefer above all is a liquor made out of millet and called *kakiat*. The quality of *kakiat* varies from area to area. Some is little better than poison, but that produced in Mairang, a small town about 25 miles from Shillong, is really more than passable and deserves to be better known.

Because of the abundance of fruit like plums, peaches and cherries, Shillong boasts of a number of connoisseurs who make their own fruit wine. These people talk expertly of tubs and vats and pipes and yeast and temperatures and sugar. The room where the production is going on is out of bounds to everyone. The owner, however, will disappear into it from time to time, and come out after having performed mysterious rites, speaking of fermentation and alcohol content. This goes on for months, till one day you are greeted by the brewer's warm smile and an invitation to partake a little something after dinner. You arrive, and are served the product of his labors in the tiniest of sherry glasses. You hold your glass up against the light, sniff delicately, swirl the contents, and then take a sip. All this while your host is regarding you with a look of the greatest concern. And when you declare yourself satisfied with the quality of his product, a smile suffuses his face as if few things are capable of giving greater pleasure to him who wants to see everybody happy.

The Khasis are also great smokers. Indeed, there is more pipe smoking in Meghalaya than I have seen in just about any other part of the country with the possible exception of Mizoram and Arunachal Pradesh. Khasi pipes are short, stubby things that smokers often carve themselves, and the tobacco that is used is strong, foul, very fast burning, and very cheap. You can see heaps of it in Bara Bazar, while standing around will be several men, each with a pipe stuck nonchalantly in his mouth.

The Khasi Hills are truly alive with the sound of music. A love for music is very widespread, and the people have a remarkable musical talent. Without any training at all the average man or woman can reproduce a simple tune perfectly after having heard it just once. Khasis have lovely voices, which is just as well because they all love to sing. Church services afford them ample opportunities for the exercise of their talents. And impromptu singsongs are always taking place. Three or four friends sitting together will sometimes just spontaneously burst into song; and on summer nights, when people can wander out of doors till late, you often hear the singing coming from all directions.

There are a few Khasi language songs, mostly of a patriotic nature, which the Khasis will sing or whistle from time to time. Hindi film songs are rather more popular. But most popular are all Western pop hits. Khasis can spend goodly sums of money on pop records and cassettes, and many possess guitars and can give very good imitations of the latest fashionable singer in the United States. It is with a desire of harnessing this interest to religious ends that several churches have started the practice of inviting singing groups to present special numbers during church service. The congregation loves it; sometimes people remember the special number they heard better than the sermon itself. They sing devotional songs set to the latest popular music and are so thrilled by the music that they hypnotize themselves into believing what the words of the song are trying to inculcate.

Given the Khasi love for, and talent in, Western popular music, I suspect that it is only a matter of time before one or another young Khasi makes a name for him or herself in popular music.

Classical Indian music has no appeal for the Khasi, and he makes little effort to develop a taste for it. The status of classical Western music is better, but only just. Some people listen to it, and a few rich Khasi families own pianos and arrange lessons for their daughters, But, considering the great love many Khasis display for all things Western, it is remarkable how little knowledge of, or interest in, this kind of music exists. Recently the government has started an Institute of Art, and Daulat Nanavati has been employed to give lessons in Western classical music. Daulat, who once worked for the Western Music Program of All India Radio, is an accomplished pianist and music teacher. She has been successful in enthusing young people, but the limited facilities of the Institute have rendered her task difficult. She makes a further point. Her students, she points out, are talented, and keen, and have a good ear. But they lack discipline or concentration. Till such time as they learn these qualities, it is unlikely that they will be able to exploit their natural gifts fully.

The Khasis have neither taken to, nor are interested in most sports played around the world. Cricket, field hockey, tennis, basketball find only a few devotees in Meghalaya. But the story is different when it comes to soccer. It is played everywhere, and very popular with spectators. The soccer team of St. Anthony's School has gained a national reputation for playing with great pluck and determination, and always reaching the quarter final stage in the annual Subroto Memorial Tournament played in Delhi. Wherever there is a bit of open ground, you will find Khasi children dribbling, kicking and heading the ball with gusto.

Soccer tournaments are held regularly between different localities in Shillong, each of which fields a team. These matches are played before vast throngs of excited supporters, and the results invariably broadcast on the 8:25 a.m. local news the next morning. Sometimes up to two minutes of the five-minute broadcast are taken up with items such as "Nongthymmai beat Malki in a scintillating finish by two goals to one."

The people of the Khasi Hills have their own indigenous sports. A love for fishing is widespread. Even more popular is archery, at which the Khasis are very good. I have seen groups of half a dozen men or so all shooting at the same target from a distance of about 200 yards with amazing skill and accuracy. Archery competitions are particularly popular in the countryside and provide an occasion for people to bet and gamble away lots of money. Indeed, the average Khasi is such an inveterate gambler that quite considerable sums were lost on races when Shillong was on the race map of India. I was told that horse racing was finally stopped largely in order to save people from ruining themselves through too great a fondness for the sport.

Khasis who have converted to Christianity celebrate only Christian festivals. But non-Christian Khasis celebrate a number of festivals and dances, as do the other tribals of India. The most important of them is the Nongkhrem Dance, which usually takes place in September or October, though sometimes it may be held as late as November. It is held at a place called Smit, about ten miles or so from Shillong on the way to Jowai.

Smit is an important place. For one thing, it is the seat of the Syiem of Nongkhrem. Syiems are Khasi rajas, but they are unlike the rajas and maharajas that India used to know till not all that long ago. The principalities of Syiems are small and they themselves are quite often unspectacular, indeed almost seedy looking individuals. Not for them the finery and pomp and the glamorous wealth that the maharajas in pre-Independence India enjoyed. Nor do they have the same powers. Their rule is strictly limited, and even in the unimportant areas of life over which they hold sway, they are obliged to follow the counsel of their advisors. The Syiemship is, in fact, a largely symbolic and ceremonial office. One of the most important ceremonies over which the Syiem of Nongkhrem presides is the annual dance.

The dance takes place in the courtyard outside his palace. As palaces go, his is a very sorry affair. But it offers some features of interest. Made entirely of wood, there is reputed to be not one iron nail in it. It is also well over a hundred years old, and may claim with some justification to be one of the oldest buildings in the Khasi Hills. The dance lasts over several days, climaxing on the last. Then all schools and colleges in Shillong are closed and everyone troops to Smit, old and young, Christian and non-Christian, local and outsider and tourist. All these people have a wonderful time around the open countryside in Smit eating at the various cheap food-and-tea stalls that spring up everywhere. But few are enthralled either by the dance or by the accompanying music.

We went to the dance one year. The music, produced on drums and a *shehnai*-like wind instrument, sounded unimaginative and monotonous to me; it didn't even have a memorable melodic line. And the dance itself was the most painfully slow and aimless shuffling of men and women I have seen. The men danced in an outer circle, the women in the inner. The men at least went round and round, though at a slow pace and without any attempt to move in time to the music. From time to time, they also whirled the whisks they carried in their hands in a half-hearted way. But the women, for the most part, moved only minimally. They just shuffled a foot or so in front, or to the side, and then shuffled back again. Every so often a dancer would get bored with what he or she was doing and just pull out. Then, talking to his or her friends, the dancer showed greater animation than was ever exhibited during the performance. Once in a while, I suppose, he or she felt a twinge of conscience at having ambled out of the dance; then the dancer ambled back again into it. Meanwhile the music played on, wailing and rather unpleasant by now. But no one minded; no one was paying much attention.

If the actual dance, so different from the vigorous and rhythmic dances of the other tribals, was a disappointment, the costumes were not. The men, it is true, were dressed rather shabbily. They wore poorly cut terylene jackets and baggy, almost shapeless yellow *dhotis*. Occasionally someone wore a tie. Their garlands were made of cheap, tinselly material, and their turbans looked grotesque. But the women were splendid. Their garments were yellow and made out of old, heavy silk. And they were laden with minor fortunes in the form of heavy 24-carat gold jewelry. Their head dresses were also made of solid gold and required constant adjustment. Perhaps it was the fear of displacing these heavy crowns that made them so slow in their movements. And occasionally—incongruous sight—a woman dancer would be accompanied by a female attendant holding an umbrella over her head.

Women dancers are quite used to being photographed and will stand still in a stiff pose whenever they see anyone with a camera. I took a few photographs and was astonished at how the dance costume and make-up transformed the ordinary Khasi girl. Generally they are vivacious and giggle a lot. But the dancer wearing her special costume had lost all facial expression and personality. She had become just a dressed-up dummy or doll with no recognition in her eyes or her blank, unlined, heavily powdered and rouged face.

The musicians and dancers were all non-Christian; many belonged to the Syiem's family. The churches prohibit their members from performing in these pagan rites; and though the occasional Christian finds this ban irksome and will even break it, by and large the Christian Khasis have given up participation in the old customs of their tribe.

At the end of the Nongkhrem Dance you may join the hundreds of people who wait patiently for buses and travel back to Shillong in the most cramped and uncomfortable conditions. Or, if you are not too tired, you may accompany the many more who walk back along a shortcut over the hills. These latter groups are in high spirits as they return. Several have imbibed liberal quantities of *kakiat* during the day and carry hip flasks to make the walk back less tiring. Many carry guitars which they strum all the way down. People burst into song; others take up the refrain. Lovers straggle behind. Several men and women link arms as they walk along, talking, shouting, giggling at jokes that are bandied about. And as it gets dark the stars appear in a clear and frosty sky, brilliant and big. Because of the clarity of the air and the altitude, the stars in Meghalaya appear bigger and brighter than in many other places. The moon is a glow behind pine trees which stand dark and silent, watching all and exuding a fresh, delicate perfume over everything. Your heart develops a yearning for it knows not what; and as this vague emotion rises like a lump in your throat, the man or woman who is walking beside you puts their arms through yours in a spontaneous gesture of acceptance and camaraderie. It is at such moments that my love for the Khasis and their land has been the keenest.

Chapter 6
WORK

IN EARLY APRIL 1974 I WAS SERVING AS HEAD OF the English Department and Dean of St. Stephen's College, Delhi, generally regraded as the preeminent liberal arts undergraduate college of India, and had got married just the previous September. I was happy, professionally as well as personally. Being both Head of Department and Dean posed challenges, but by now I had learnt the ropes and was managing quite well. In fact, I had just begun to feel that a little spicing up of life might not be a bad thing when Prabhu Guptara dropped in one day. Prabhu had been a student and had recently got a job as English lecturer at the newly founded North-Eastern Hill University in Shillong.

Prabhu managed to convince me to apply for a job there. The place, he said, was idyllic, the climate cool, and the new university offered the freedom I had always craved to devise new courses, teach in new ways, and try out new ways of assessing students. So I applied, was interviewed for a professorship, and offered a Readership. I should probably have refused—I had refused a Readership at Delhi University just two years previously in favor of the Headship and Deanship at St. Stephen's. But the Vice Chancellor, who was a very persuasive man, said that though a Reader, I would be paid the salary I should have received as a full professor. Moreover, there was a very good chance of Frances getting a job at NEHU. Finally, he gave me a verbal assurance that he would ask the University Grants Commission to sanction a second full professorship which would then be mine. I was sold, and accepted. The professorship for which I had applied went to Dr. A.G. George, a Reader in Delhi whom I knew slightly.

In some ways the move to Shillong proved fruitful; in others it was a disappointment. The promised professorship never materialized and left me feeling bitter. Shortly after arriving in Shillong, I went to see Dr. Devanesen, only to be told that he was away in Delhi. After a number of attempts I finally managed an appointment, but when I brought up the subject of my promised professorship, he became vague. He had asked for the creation of another professorship, he said, but didn't think that it would be sanctioned. Anyhow, he would try again. When I asked him again a few weeks later, he looked uncomfortable and said that I was receiving a professor's salary, so what was the hurry in getting that title as well? A few other meetings were equally infructuous, and I realized that his early assurance to me was not going to be honored.

I swallowed this rather unpalatable truth, but it rankled the whole time I was in Shillong and I lost some of my early respect for Devanesen.

After our first year there, my wife applied for a lectureship, was interviewed, and appointed. But now a hitch developed. Dr. Devanesen informed us that because she was not Indian, special permission would be required from the Home Ministry for her to be allowed to teach. We kept waiting for this permission, but it did not come. My suspicion is that Devanesen never applied for it. It was sheer serendipity that this topic came up one day during a conversation with Mr. Rustomji. He said nothing, but I guess that he must have got on the phone to the Home Ministry in Delhi, for the following week Frances received a letter from a Deputy Secretary saying that she had been granted permission.

So she got a job in the English Department too, and we were able to live comfortably in a large house with a wonderful landlord. Khasi society, we found, could be worse even than provincial, being centered around small tribal concerns. But there were many men and women of wide culture in Shillong, and so we did not lack for stimulating company. I have already mentioned the friends we made with government officials at all levels from the Chief Secretary down; and we got to know plenty of educated Khasis and men and women of other tribes who inhabit Shillong, mixed freely and frequently with our colleagues in the university without, however, making any close or lasting friendships, and often interacted with other men and women in Shillong like businessmen, booksellers, small merchants, and ordinary Khasis. Above all, we got to know and become very attached to our students. They were uniformly sweet. Some were as bright as any. A majority was able to read and write English competently and was not without ability. They were willing to work hard, but they had not been taught to develop rigor in their thought and did not always push their minds far enough. We used to say that the best students were as good as the best in Delhi, though there were fewer of them; the other students would neither stand out in Delhi nor disgrace themselves. Where they truly excelled was as human beings. Open, generous, fresh, welcoming, receptive, respectful, and full of fun, they were as fine a group of young men and women as one could meet anywhere.

The university to which we went, the North-Eastern Hill University, had been established in 1972 in order to meet the aspirations of a region of the country that had been historically marginalized if not totally neglected. The university had jurisdiction over two recently-created States that were populated almost entirely by tribal people, Meghalaya and Nagaland, and the Union Territory of Arunachal Pradesh. People in the rest of India knew very little about those who inhabited this area, and unflattering stereotypes abounded. It was known, of course, that there was an insurgency of long standing among the Nagas, and perhaps the Mizo insurgency had also seeped into the national consciousness. More than that much of India did not know, and most people didn't care.

NEHU's primary task was to bring a high quality of higher education to this region. The idea was not to do here what was being done in universities round the country and do it less well, but rather to help the rest of India to understand the history and culture of the tribes who lived here while also training the minds of their youth, making them qualified for a variety of jobs, and bringing them into the national mainstream. For this purpose, it was envisaged that research would be undertaken in local flora and fauna, in anthropology, linguistics, history, sociology, music, economic and political structures, and other such areas. The presence of the university would provide a fillip to regional arts and letters, and the university would also help bring into this hitherto isolated area books, ideas, methods of work and of inquiry from the rest of the country and indeed the whole world. The university would thus facilitate a two-way intellectual transfer. We, the faculty, were there to transmit knowledge and encourage research in our own fields and disciplines, but we were also there to imbibe knowledge from local people and in the process widen the scope of our own research and posit new ways of inquiry into the nature of things.

The man chosen to translate this ideal into reality was the Vice Chancellor. Chandran Devanesen had a Ph.D. from Harvard; his dissertation, which was subsequently published and still gets cited by scholars, was on Gandhi. A Christian, when appointed to NEHU he was serving as a highly successful and popular Principal of the Madras Christian College; and apart from his distinguished academic qualifications and administrative experience, one reason he was chosen for the position was that the north-east is largely Christian, and they wanted a Christian in that position in order to achieve greater acceptability among the locals.

Devanesen was bright, cultured, articulate, energetic, entirely cosmopolitan, and full of ideas that were original and creative. Unfortunately, he was not able to implement most of them. One of his drawbacks was that he allowed the perks of office to go to his head. In those early days of NEHU's founding it was necessary for him to go to Delhi frequently for meetings, for interviews, and to hire staff. Sometimes he would be away for days, but more often he would return to Shillong for a day or two before flying off to Delhi again, with the result that there were times when he flew between Delhi and Shillong three times a week. He began to think that the more time he spent in the air, the more highly he was going to be regarded not just by his faculty and students but also by the bigwigs of the Education ministry. What he did not realize was that these frequent absences from his desk were also deleterious to the affairs of the university, for while he was in Delhi hobnobbing with the powerful, work would be piling up back in Shillong and blocking progress while important decisions remained pending.

Maybe it wouldn't have been so bad had he had a strong team of people in Shillong to manage in his absence. But another of his problems was that he was a mediocre judge of people. Though Devanesen made a few very good appointments—the chief librarian B.V. Kesavan, whom I shall turn to presently, was one—several of his top lieutenants were badly chosen.

One such person was his chief of staff, as it were, who had the title of Officer on Special Duty for administration; he was a Mizo government official from the Posts and Telegraphs department named Towcchaung. Another such person was his chief financial officer, another government official from Bihar, Boipai.

Towchhaung was, in some respects, a grand man. If you visited him at home, he could be most hospitable and friendly and welcoming, and my wife and I spent some very pleasant evenings with him and his family. But, in his office, he held court. You went into his office because you had important business to transact, and you would find half a dozen other colleagues, supplicants all, sitting across from his desk drinking tea. Tea would be ordered for you, and then Towcchaung might throw you a crumb or two of conversation, ask you about your family, or whether you had heard the latest news. He would hold forth on whatever subject was of interest to him at that moment, and if you brought up your own concerns, he would cut you short. Maybe after half an hour of this, he might ask you to state your business, but even then he would not address it. Other people had got there before you; their demands had to be considered, or a phone had to be answered, or a file signed. Discouraged, you would go home, only to return the following day and go through the same routine. Eventually you would be able to transact your business, but not before you had been made to feel that you were a supplicant, a mere worm to whom a favor had been granted by the great man. The university was new, administrative systems were still being set up, and it was necessary to approach Towcchaung for every small thing; and no matter how legitimate your business, he always made you feel this way. I used to have to go to see him frequently, and though I liked him, I used to hate these visits. They were an affront to my dignity and my position, and they resulted in a colossal waste of time. Many other people felt like I did, but no one spoke out, and Dr. Devanesen, oblivious of the true state of affairs, did nothing to get rid of Towcchaung.

Only students had the power to deal with his lofty high handedness. Winters in Shillong are cold, and in Mayurbhanj Palace, where we used to conduct classes, there was a fireplace in the classroom which came in very useful. But the coal had to be sanctioned by Towcchaung, and one winter he did not do so. In the meanwhile, it got colder and colder, and appeals to him produced no results. Finally the students took matters into their own hands. They piled up some classroom desks and chairs in the fireplace and set them on fire. The next day there was coal waiting to be burned.

Boipai was another story. He was in charge of financial matters. He was a man of few words and fewer actions. Bills and invoices would go to his office and disappear into a dark hole, remaining unpaid for months. He had an incompetent staff over whom he did not seem to exercise any control. The man responsible for our salaries was someone called Wallang. At the end of my first year of service I was due for an increment, so I was very surprised to see that my salary had actually gone down. I went to see Wallang and he blithely informed me that since I had got an increment, he had deducted that amount from my salary. The man did not understand that an increment meant that he had to add that amount to, not deduct it from, my salary.

No wonder the accounts of the university soon turned into an unholy mess. Eventually, Boipai was fired and the auditor who came to set things right informed us that some of the money that was missing had been stolen and the rest lost due to incompetent and incorrect accounting practices. All this happened under Devanesen's watch, but he did not know and, when he discovered it, he was loath to get rid of Boipai till his hand was forced.

Devanesen made some other bad appointments. I am, of course, biased, but I never thought that the Head of the English department, Dr. George, ought to have been appointed to that position. He had been a Reader at Delhi, where he enjoyed a somewhat mixed reputation. He was respected for his scholarship, and he had published a number of books, including on T.S. Eliot, John Milton and Soren Kierkegaard. But he was also temperamental, played favorites, lacked balance or clear judgment, and could be high-handed, though at other times he was all sweetness and light. I had assumed that I would be made a full professor, but that never happened and instead Dr. George was not only appointed a full professor but also the Head of the department. I thought that my claims were as strong as his, and inevitably tension developed between us, which did not conduce to a happy relationship.

George struck me as an insecure man, highly unsure of himself. He used to be known as A.G. George, but after about a year or two at NEHU he decided that he would revert to his original Malayali name, which was A.G. Ghevarghese. He had announced that the year of his birth was 1926; he later began to say that that had been a mistake and it was really 1929. He was clearly nervous of both Frances and me. I thought he was intimidated by our supposedly better educational qualifications and believed that we always criticized or laughed at him behind his back. He was not wrong, for we did. For instance, we found it hilarious that when he met female students, he would ask them if they were nice, meaning if they were well. "Nice" in this context was not merely incorrect; it could be put to the wrong kind of interpretation. But he didn't seem to notice. For his part, he did not like us at all. Frances also thought that he was a misogynist. He was a bachelor and seemed to get on well with women students both in and out of the classroom. But in private his comments on some of them did him no credit. There was a time when rumor was rife that he might marry a Garo student. Nothing came of it, but I remember his once referring to her as a Garo elephant because she was a little heavy. He avoided the female members of the department when he could; certainly, he did not socialize with them as he tended to do with other men. And he had no ideas about educational reform. Frances and I were keen to create new syllabi and methods of assessment, but he thought that the best we could do was to implement a slightly watered-down version of the Delhi University M.A. syllabus for NEHU. In the event, that is what happened. My high hopes and grand plans came to nothing. I'll have something more to say about syllabus making a little later on.

Dr. Hom Chaudhuri was the other Reader, and because he had joined before I did, was considered senior to me. In some ways he was a pathetic creature, and in other ways a laughable one. He had taught in a college in Shillong and had obtained a Ph.D. on Shakespeare, but his scholarship was outmoded, his critical approach belletristic, and his lectures were little more than emotional, high-pitched perorations full of repetitions and signifying little. You could not help overhearing what he was saying as you passed by his classroom. "The lamb, the lamb, the lamb!" he would shout. "Who made you, the poet asks, who made you, who made you? God, God, God, says the poet; God made the little lamb, God made him." And thus was Blake taught by Hom Chaudhuri.

He was gawky and nervous in his manner. He knew that people laughed at him behind his back, and that made him touchy and resentful as well and quick to quarrel. Both he and George suffered from a deep-seated inferiority complex, and so it was in a sense natural for them to team up and find support in each other. But they also distrusted each other. Hom Chaudhuri, let it be said to his credit, never bad-mouthed George, but George would often recount little anecdotes of Hom Chaudhuri's ignorance or absurdities. As for me, I treated Hom Chaudhuri with contempt and George with some envy mixed with some contempt. With things being like this between the three senior members of the department, it is easy to imagine that the atmosphere was usually one of some tension and distrust. The remarkable thing is that we were still able to pull along well enough, and keep the students out of this loop of hostility and friction successfully enough, for their education not to suffer; indeed, we were even able to make a few improvements in the way they were educated.

I would ascribe this fact to various reasons. First, for all the tension or, at any rate, distrust that existed among the three of us, we were each concerned enough about the welfare of students, the integrity of the department and of the subject that we were professing, and of the need to make sure that NEHU succeeded, to put our animosities aside and cooperate for the common good. I would say that this was because we were basically men of good will, and also because each of us was imbued with a sense of common purpose that grew out of all of us teaching English and valuing what we were doing. There was something about the nature of the discipline itself that made us committed to a set of values where the larger good took precedence over self. I wonder whether this would have happened as easily in any other academic department, or whether there was something special to professing English that brought this about, something that made us examine our motives more carefully, take stock of our actions, and decide that no matter how much we disliked one another, we had to pull our weight.

Second, the presence of two or three junior members of the department acted as a wholly salutary influence. Noorul Hasan was the first person appointed to the faculty in NEHU. He had a First Class M.A. from

Allahabad from the days when Allahabad could boast the strongest English department between Delhi and Calcutta, with stalwarts like Professor Deb and Raghupati Sahai "Firaq," perhaps the greatest Urdu poet of the twentieth century after Iqbal, on the faculty. Noorul started teaching in St. John's, Agra, in 1964, which is where I first met him one summer vacation when I was back from Oxford. I was told that a bright young spark had joined the English department, and so I went to see him and make his acquaintance. He was down with typhoid, stretched out in bed, thin and weak, and immersed in a collection of Hardy's poems. When I returned to teach in St. Stephen's, Delhi, he was teaching at Kirori Mal College and living in Gwyer Hall, and we became good friends and met frequently and talked, till one day he suddenly disappeared. Rumors began circulating that he had got married, but no one knew where he had gone. And there he was in the English department when I turned up in Shillong. I was glad to renew our old friendship and we saw quite a lot of each other in my first year there. But the following year he won a Commonwealth Scholarship to Manchester, from where he returned after four years with a Ph.D. and a brilliant dissertation on Hardy, subsequently published, just as Frances and I were getting ready to leave Shillong. So though I consider Noorul an old and dear friend, we did not serve as colleagues in Shillong for more than a year. His sane presence played a part in keeping the department functioning well in spite of all the problems between George, Hom Chaudhuri and myself.

Prabhu Guptara was the second person after Noorul to be appointed to the NEHU faculty. He was a first year student in the B.A. Pass class of St. Stephen's in my first year of teaching there. He was so plainly overqualified for that class that a colleague, Dan O'Connor, and I prevailed upon the Principal to let Prabhu move into the Honors class at the beginning of his second year. Prabhu graduated with a good Second Class degree, went on to do an M.A. in Delhi, and earned a reputation in college as an earnest follower of Jesus Christ, but above all as a good man. It was he who, on a visit to Delhi from Shillong, persuaded me to apply for a position at NEHU, and I was very glad that he would be a colleague there. He, too, contributed to the smooth functioning of the department, but the year after Noorul left for Manchester, Prabhu went off to Stirling University in Scotland for a Ph.D.

Noorul and Prabhu were replaced by others, most of them good. Paul Pimomo was a Naga who joined us just after he graduated, first as a research student under George's supervision and later as a lecturer on the faculty. Friendly, sane, balanced, mature, and, being a tribal, capable of understanding our tribal students' needs and desires from the inside, as it were, he was a good acquisition. Temsula Ao was another Naga who, though somewhat older and with a young family, threw herself into the life of the department fully, had a great rapport with students, and taught effectively. Juanita War was a Khasi who joined the department after having taught English for some years at one of the women's colleges in Shillong. She was serious and could be somewhat aloof, but was quite successful in the classroom.

Anjana Desai joined us as the third Reader in the department in the second year of my stay there. We became friends, though I had my problems with her. She had a Ph.D. from Cornell and had taught in Surat. She was competent, always well prepared for her classes, gave a great deal of herself to her students, and became thoroughly involved in the life of the department and the university. She was universally liked. But early in her stay at NEHU she developed the notion that George was up to something that might either hurt or help her, and in order to better read his mind and ensure that no harm, only good, would come to her from any actions he might take, decided to stick to him like a leech. Wherever he went she was sure to follow. If she could not go to a meeting or conference where he was present, she would cotton on to him as soon as he came out to try and pump what information she could about what had transpired. George, I think, was both flattered by this constant attendance and also irritated by it. As I said, he might well have been a misogynist, and this being followed around everywhere and being fawned on by a woman was not anything he welcomed, though he wouldn't shake her off because it pleased his vanity. I found Anjana's behavior demeaning, and it rather put me off her, though we continued to be friends.

There is some truth in the view that, like a doctor's office, an academic department is only as good as its secretary. Not only does s/he manage all the paperwork, etc., not only is s/he the repository of such confidential information as might need to be preserved, but s/he is often the face of the department, the first person a visitor is likely to meet; and often the impression s/he gets of the secretary carries over into his/her final judgement of the department. Our secretary was Beatrice Nichol, never called by her first name but always referred to as Mrs. Nichol. Tall, thin, with the demeanor of a person who has suffered adversities and is beaten down, she almost always wore a Mizo wraparound skirt called a *puan*, and a blouse or a shirt. She was the daughter of a British tea planter, now deceased, and a Bihari tribal mother who lived with her in a big, rambling house that her father had left them, near the Polo Ground. As a secretary she was so-so. She knew how to type and take shorthand dictation, though she was not particularly good at either skill, filed papers, and did Dr. George's bidding. Faculty were in and out of her office all the time, sometimes on business, at other times just because they had some time to kill; and she was always pleasant with them though her conversation was all about trivia. She got along well with all the students also, while making sure that she did not discuss with them anything that they were not supposed to know. For the rest, she kept her counsel and offered no opinion on anything. Perhaps she had nothing to say. She had a younger sister, Ena, a good-looking, bright and vivacious young woman who became our student and earned a respectable degree. When last heard of, she was hoping to get a lectureship in one of the local colleges. I believe she had also had a baby.

We visited the sisters at home on a few occasions. We met the mother, who was a quiet lady and generally kept herself to herself. It was quite obvious that maintaining the house was getting to be difficult. What struck us most was the furniture and decorations of the living room. Mr. Nichol had obviously been a great hunter while in Assam. There were stools made out of the feet of elephants he had shot. There was a stuffed crocodile in a glass cage. The walls were decorated with antlers and deer heads. In an adjoining room, behind a curtain, was the *piece de resistance*: a stuffed Bengal tiger. I've never been closer to a tiger than to that one; and though dead and stuffed, it still retained its ferocity.

Mrs. Nichol had an office assistant, a young Khasi man named Godfrey. He was enthusiastic, friendly, helpful, obliging, and always willing to carry out such tasks, light as they were, as were assigned to him. One weekend he went fishing to Barapani with a group of friends, and most tragically was drowned. The news grieved every one of us greatly and filled us with sorrow. He was a good man who had a future ahead of him.

The university consisted of two buildings, though some more were built towards the end of my tenure there. The horseshoe building in La Chaumiere was three stories high and, keeping its shape in mind, was aptly named. It housed the offices of the Vice Chancellor, Towcchaung, Boipai, the Controller of Exams, a retired gentleman from Kerala called C.C. David who was friendly, conducted his business fairly and efficiently, and kept out of university politics and squabbling and back biting. Teaching was carried on in a palace which had originally belonged to the royal family of Mayurbhanj, a princely state in Orissa, and been requisitioned by the government because the family had failed to pay taxes. It was quite a grand edifice. Two of the bedrooms became our two classrooms for the M. A. Previous and Final classes. A large dressing room became the office of the Head of the English Department, and another hall-like room next door the office of the Secretary of the department. Various other rooms were allocated to faculty as offices. I shared the *puja* room, right on top of the porch, with Frances and one or two other teachers. I had a glorious view of the drive up to the palace plus small clusters of Khasi pines on either side. Down the road, in a number of buildings on the side, were the departments of Botany and Chemistry, together with their labs. The billiards room downstairs was the original library; when the number of books increased, the library was moved upstairs to a larger area. The palace kitchen was where a few *kongs* set up their tea business from where they kept us all supplied with endless cups of tea.

The palace had certain unique features. Apparently at one time it was the home of two small children who were absolutely inseparable, and so their parents built them a room with an attached bathroom which had two of everything: two toilets side by side, two wash basins, two bathtubs. On the whole we managed to get along quite well in a building clearly not meant as the academic wing of a university.

My work consisted of teaching only M.A. classes. Because there were not more than forty or fifty students in all, and five or six faculty members, student-teacher relations were close, and we got to know many students socially, and in some cases their families as well. They would visit us at home, and we them. It became possible for us to hold occasional poetry readings in our house, and in two years of the four that we spent in Shillong, my wife and I were involved in two theatrical productions as well. One year she directed the medieval *Second Shepherd's Play* at Christmas, and another year I played the hero in Vijay Tendulkar's *Sakharam Binder* opposite the wife of a colleague and with other cast members consisting only of students; the director was Noorul.

These social interactions with students afforded much pleasure.

Maybe a word or two about these plays may not be out of order. Unfortunately, because of a mix-up with dates we missed the performance of the *Second Shepherd's Play*, though Frances saw it through all the rehearsals. *Sakharam Binder* was altogether a much more ambitious venture. We spent a whole semester rehearsing and learning our lines. There were going to be two performances in a public theatre, and tickets were going to be sold. When word got out that we were putting on this play, a number of people in town, particularly rather straitlaced church members, objected. It was supposed to be a play which inculcated "bad morals," it was alleged, and might be harmful to the young. It is true that the play is about a man who has a mistress and then brings another woman home; eventually he murders the second woman and the first helps him bury her because the killing has made the man lose all resolve and the first woman knows that she will be able to dominate him henceforth. But in no way is it an immoral play, and I was glad that the Vice Chancellor as well as the other functionaries of the university upheld our right to stage it.

The role of the second woman was performed by Sujata Miri, the wife of Mrinal Miri whom I had known at St. Stephen's, Delhi, and who was now the Head of the Philosophy department at NEHU in which his wife Sujata was a Reader. The first night was a success. Everything went well on the second night of the performance till the end when the woman Sujata was playing is killed. As she lay there, acting the part of a corpse, she realized that her sari had perhaps been pushed too far up, whereupon the corpse moved, pulled the sari down, and then became a corpse again. This was supposed to be the tragic climax of the play; instead, laughter rang to the rafters.

The smallness of our numbers made it possible to devote plenty of personal attention to students' academic needs in class. The tutorial system, which the department tried to introduce, never really took off: many teachers were not familiar with what was entailed and turned the hour into a *viva voce* session, or gave mini lectures, and many students, thinking that tutorials were little more than coaching classes which were an established tradition in Shillong, came unprepared. I realized how lucky I was to have taken to the system naturally, first as a student at Oxford and then a teacher at St. Stephen's. For it is a delicate plant, not easily transplanted to any or every kind of cultural soil. Looking back, it is remarkable that it flourished so well at St. Stephen's. It takes a certain kind of tutor to make it work, and the student has to do his or her share too, in the form of not only having an essay ready every week but also of possessing a curious, questing, skeptical intelligence and enjoying the give and take of argument and debate. Students in Shillong were receptive to new ideas but did not necessarily possess enough of their own, and so tutorial sessions became occasions for them to absorb rather than to defend, question and argue.

I fear that some of my feelings of frustration must have spilled over in tutorial sessions. I used to ask students at the end of the year to respond anonymously to a questionnaire that sought to elicit their views of my teaching. Such student evaluation of faculty is neither required in educational institutions in India nor generally undertaken on a voluntary basis by the teachers. For precisely this reason I valued the comments I received; and while many were gratifying, there were also two or three students who found me to be overbearing, condescending or abrasive. I suspect that these were the students who resented my pushing them or their classmates too hard or too relentlessly, questioning them too sharply, and expressing my views too bluntly. These students had a critical sense all right, but needed the cloak of anonymity in order to express it rather than letting it show in the give and take of tutorials to which they were not accustomed.

Lecture classes were small and it was therefore possible, instead of lecturing impersonally to large numbers of anonymous students, as I was to do later in Delhi, to speak to each one of them. At any rate, this is what I strove for. I also continued to improve my lecturing techniques that I had developed first in St. John's and then at St. Stephen's. I was able to hold students' attention a good deal of the time, and to combine, more or less satisfactorily, a discussion of individual texts, including close reading of selected passages, with a commentary on larger historical, social or aesthetic issues. I tried to enlarge students' familiarity with cultural issues, provide knowledge about authors and their works, and supply a model as well as the necessary apparatus for analyzing and interrogating texts, making comparisons, and arriving at judgments, all the while not ignoring the exigencies of exams.

Exams could not be forgotten in Shillong, as they cannot anywhere else in India. We tried to make them count for less by assigning part of the final grade to "internal assessment," meaning work done by the student throughout the year in the form of tutorials, but eventually this assessment came to mean little more than the aggregate of grades received in class quizzes and short answer tests. Given the situation in the rest of the country, even this was an improvement. Students could only deepen their familiarity with the material they studied if they had to take these periodical tests. I tried to cast my tools for internal assessment in the form of multiple-choice exams. I was brought up to regard this type of exam with skepticism, but learned in trying to make some that the proper crafting of these tests is a minor art in itself. I made them as factual and textual as I could, thus ensuring that the students knew at least some of the little facts and details about given works—dates, prosodic features, stanza forms, rhyme schemes, influences—and this way freed myself to set essay-type questions in the final that would test the examinees' writing skills and organizational and critical abilities. I came to the disconcerting realization that while they were able to write their essay-type questions not too badly, they had difficulty with multiple choice questions. Either they were not trained for this type of test, or, as appeared more likely, essay-type questions gave them the opportunity to waffle or perorate a little, thus concealing their ignorance in verbiage, while multiple choice questions required an exactness of knowledge that they did not always possess. I think I had only two or three students in the four years I taught in Shillong who answered multiple choice tests with distinction, though plenty of students did well in essay type questions.

One reason many students in Shillong knew so little was because they didn't read much outside the prescribed textbooks. Those who wished to know more were often stonewalled by the fact that there were no decent libraries in town, the public library being largely devoted to cultural shows, and college libraries being very inadequate. The university had set up a brand-new library when my wife and I joined. Unfortunately we didn't have a good librarian, nor was the library staff well trained. They seemed to think that because books looked neat when nicely shelved, they should remain shelved that way all the time, and got upset when a student or teacher pulled books out to read or left them on tables. The gaps this caused on the shelves looked unsightly, and that the staff could not tolerate. Therefore, they were not very happy issuing books out, for if books were taken away for a period of time, the shelves would look bare, and that would never do.

Their cataloguing system was just as bizarre as their attitude towards letting books be used. We didn't know whether to be shocked or amused when R.K. Narayan's novel *The Maneater of Malgudi* was classified under the category of Wildlife and placed next to Jim Corbett's classic *The Maneater of Kumaon*.

Therefore, we were all very pleased when Dr. Kesavan joined us as NEHU's Chief Librarian. He was the author of an authoritative study of printing in India, and had served as Director of the National Library of Calcutta. He was big, he was stentorian, and he could be gruff, impatient and intimidating. I was delighted, since I thought that these qualities needed to be much exercised if the library were to be set on an even keel. And he was the right man to do so, for he was forward looking, knowledgeable, dynamic, brooked no nonsense, and enjoyed direct access to Dr. Devanesen , which meant that he wouldn't have to kowtow to Towcchaung and drink endless cups of tea before he could achieve anything.

Not that he was averse to drinking tea or anything stronger. Every morning at about half past ten a few of us faculty members would get together with him and Dr. Guha, our resident medical officer, for a round of tea and gossip. Actually these gossip sessions were more in the nature of seminars, except that no one led them. It was a free for all discussion group where ideas about the university were the main topic of conversation, but each of us talked about the work we were engaged in, the classes we were teaching and our ideas for teaching them, what we had learned about the culture, traditions, music, food habits, etc. of the tribespeople of the area, forthcoming trips, our travel experiences, ecology, history, the comings and goings of the Vice Chancellor, plays that we might consider putting up. If the weather was nice we'd all sit out in the sun, but if it was raining we would usually meet in Dr. Kesavan's office. These daily sessions were extremely important not only in the education of all of us but also in helping to create a bond between a heterogeneous group of people who represented all parts of India and a great variety of academic disciplines. I cannot help feeling, in fact, that it was in these informal tea and gossip sessions that the true foundations of a unified and coherent educational enterprise were laid.

Dr. Kesavan unwittingly found himself performing another function. Because the library was located in Mayurbhanj House, which is where teaching took place, whereas the administrative offices were about two miles away in the horseshoe-shaped building in La Chaumiere, and because Dr. Kesavan was the oldest and most senior of us all, he became not only a kind of father figure but also a substitute for the Vice Chancellor, as it were. We took our problems to him, and he became everybody's informal advisor and confessor. There was no such thing as counseling in those days in Indian universities. Students turned to their families, friends and teachers for guidance and counsel, and we the teachers began to turn to Dr. Kesavan when we needed anything of the sort. He had not thought, when he accepted the Chief Librarianship, that he would also have to be weighed down with worry about the welfare of junior colleagues, but this is what happened. It was thanks to his occasional interposing that the English department remained constantly functional and its work streamlined, in spite of our occasional bickering and tensions.

The library needed to be built up, and my wife and I, together with a number of other faculty members, were asked to draw up lists of books to be ordered. We went to town. High on our list were the works of major authors from all periods of British literature in standard editions, together with important critical works on each. But we did not ignore American literature or several minor authors. Also prominent on the list were books in English by Indian authors, translations into English of works in the regional languages, and such books as had been written in the local tribal languages, mainly Khasi.

We found that making lists was one thing, getting books another. A significant number were American publications which were simply not available in India; the same was true of several, though not nearly as many, British publications. Bookstores in Shillong and Gauhati, through which our orders were usually processed, confessed their inability to procure them, and though Calcutta booksellers proved more helpful, Calcutta was a long way off and even they were not always successful. So many of our orders remained unmet. In the meanwhile, those bookstores that had unsold texts or critical works found this to be a marvelous opportunity to unload them on the library, whether the faculty wanted or needed those books or not. The result was that the library grew, but not necessarily in the directions we had planned for it. I wonder sometimes what it is like now, whether it is used more than it was in our time, whether some of our orders have finally been filled, or whether it continues to be a dumping ground for booksellers. I also wonder what the users think of the collection, whether they are grateful to find there the material they need, or whether they complain of its inadequacies and ask why those who were responsible for stocking it in its earliest days failed in their responsibility.

My wife and I were also active in curriculum framing. This was an opportunity I had looked for when I left Delhi for the Shillong job. But when I got down to it, I realized that there were all kinds of constraints which

I would have to work with. First, it was agreed on all hands—and I was a party to this understanding—that after two years of study the student should have read at least one or two representative works by the major authors of British literature. Notions of "major" writers and the sanctity of the canon were far more fixed in my mind then than they are now, and they were even more firmly fixed in the minds of my colleagues. So a syllabus that sought to replace, say, P.B. Shelley with Mary Shelley, or Keats with Walter Savage Landor, or Hardy by Gissing was inconceivable. Second, the "representative" works had also to be accessible, meaning not only that they had to be within range of the average student's financial ability, but they also had to exist in editions that were readily available. For this reason it was considered all right to include all of Blake's *Songs of Innocence and of Experience* in the syllabus but not any of his prophetic books. Third, there had to be faculty available to teach the authors that were included in the syllabus. We were a small department and had our own different specializations. The exigencies of teaching in the Indian college system had made us all pretty versatile; thus, though my dissertation was in late Victorian and Edwardian theory, I sometimes taught Chaucer and Donne and Milton as well as eighteenth and nineteenth century poetry and, at a pinch, Restoration drama. Even so, no one could claim that he or she could teach everything, and certain authors like Richardson, Sterne and Joyce had to be left out of the syllabus because they found no takers, though everyone greatly lamented their exclusion.

Finally, the syllabus could not be created without consideration of the final exam. For examination as well as pedagogical purposes the syllabus, which was chronologically arranged, starting from Chaucer and ending with Yeats, was divided into eight papers, of which students would study four in their first year and four in the second. At the end of each year they would be examined in the papers they had studied. Each exam had therefore to contain questions on each author who was included in the syllabus for that paper. Since each exam was three hours long and required students to write three or four essay-type answers, one on each author (or, if the question required a comparison, on two authors), it meant that even though a paper might contain, say, ten authors, it was possible for the student to get away by studying only four or five, that is, just half the syllabus or less. That being so, it was pointless cramming papers with more and more authors: students would just study a selected few and ignore all the others.

Working within these constraints we produced what I think was a reasonable syllabus which gave the student a good exposure to several British authors of all periods. To do more would have required a change in the system for which the department was not prepared. It would have required jettisoning some of the eight papers and replacing them with elective or optional papers that were either genre-based or dealt with literatures other than British or covered special topics or in-depth study of authors not covered by the syllabus. Something would have been gained had we done this, but something would have been lost as well: students would have gained specialized or detailed knowledge of certain areas, but remained ignorant of others. A trade-off was involved, and we were too conservative in the mid-seventies to make it.

Realizing that the tutorial system had not really taken, I wanted to try out something else: teaching and assessing students on the lines of a typical American seminar class. Each student would be responsible for writing a paper and leading a class discussion on an author or text selected in advance. Two or three such papers would be required from each student in the seminar class, plus a quiz or exam. At the end of the semester each student would write a longer term-paper on a larger topic, based on primary and secondary reading. The final assessment would be made on the basis of all these papers and exams plus the student's class participation. Unfortunately, this scheme was never tried out. It was quite obvious that our students were not capable of reading texts on their own but needed classroom instruction, and one longer or a handful of short texts per author was as much as they could manage. In any case, the library was not rich enough to support the kind of work I was proposing.

Eventually we were able to implement a more rigorous form of this system in the Delhi M. Phil course, but I wonder whether it, or a variant thereof, has ever been tried at the M.A. level anywhere in India.

In my second, or was it third year, at NEHU the teachers decided to form a union along the lines of the Delhi University Teachers' Association, So NEHUTA was born. Elections were held, and Mrinal Miri the philosopher was elected President unopposed. However, he had to make a speech laying out his agenda. It was perhaps the most extraordinary electioneering speech I have ever heard. He said that as a philosopher he would not only practice ethical conduct but judge each issue by ethical standards. His job would be to ensure that all decisions that were made either by NEHUTA or by university administrators adhered to ethical principles; indeed, he was standing for the election because he saw it as an ethical imperative. Not a word was spoken about what he hoped to achieve for the faculty in his new position or about any impending problems that he hoped to solve. I was elected to the Executive Committee.

We held a number of meetings, but I cannot remember whether we did anything at all. Ours was a committee of much talk and no action whatever. However, from time to time piddling little matters would come up that required us to vote. On one such occasion Mrinal insisted on voting twice, once as a faculty member, and the second time as President of

NEHUTA. He put forward a philosophical argument to support his double voting which convinced nobody, but nobody particularly minded because the matter on which we were voting was of so little importance. Thus was NEHUTA run in its earliest years.

Though we saw the function of the M.A. syllabus as being the training of students to be Jacks of all fields in our discipline without being masters of any, and though we on the faculty were ourselves, as I have mentioned, reasonably adept at teaching a number of periods, genres and authors and could therefore be called, with some justification, Jacks of all trades, many of us had specializations as well. I had colleagues who had earned Ph.D.s on subjects ranging from medieval literature to nineteenth-century fiction, and some who had published on topics as varied as Milton, Eliot and Kierkegaard. Shillong gave me the opportunity to move away from the area of my dissertation and develop new interests. I published a couple of essays on contemporary Indian poetry in English in a new literary journal started by the poet Jayant Mahapatra, and became a fairly regular reviewer of books, mostly on Indian literature, for the newly started *Indian Book Chronicle*. As a graduate student I had written several essays on Milton; now I was able to revise them, write one or two more, and publish the collection in book form with Macmillan, India. Thanks to a subvention from the University Grants Commission my dissertation was also published as a book by the same publishers. Both received favorable though not extensive reviews in India; my dissertation-turned-book was also noticed by *Choice*. They received minimal notice outside India, largely because the publishers did not publicize them abroad or make them available to reviewers and libraries. It is all the more surprising therefore that there are actually a few libraries in various parts of the world that have them on their shelves; my Milton book, as I was to discover much later, also received a very fair review in *Milton Quarterly*. Neither made me any money at all, and both have long since gone out of print and, for all I know, been remaindered. Even so, Shillong impelled me to publish in a way that St. Stephen's might perhaps not have.

There was another direction in which my professional vision expanded. The Central Institute of English and Foreign Languages, headquartered in Hyderabad, opened a branch in Shillong and its faculty established close links with the English department. Though lang-lit tensions would surface from time to time, and we tended to be unnecessarily dismissive of "language-*wallahs*," many of whom were very fine teachers and scholars, and we were conscious of what they contributed. Realizing that though university English departments such as ours, or the one in St. Stephen's, enrolled students who were proficient in the English language, most school and college English departments in the country did not have this luxury, the Central Institute of English had devised courses in such pedagogically crucial areas as teaching English as a second or foreign language, teaching writing, teaching English for special purposes, conversational English, and so on. Theirs was, in fact, yeoman work; and though I did not think that most of my students had need of their services, it was obvious that the Institute's services were a boon to the local colleges as well as to those of our students who were planning to go in for English teaching as a career. Rubbing shoulders with the Institute's faculty on a daily basis afforded me an opportunity, however slight and haphazard, for becoming aware of problems confronting the profession that I had not hitherto recognized.

It was while I was at Shillong that I also began to develop an all-India perspective on some of the issues confronting my profession. The University Grants Commission organized a seminar at NEHU, attended by professors from all over the country, on the modernization of English syllabi, and I got an opportunity to hear what was going on in the rest of the country. On other occasions, I went as a delegate to conferences held in places like Hyderabad, where I was able to visit both Osmania University and the new Central University, the Central Institute of English and Foreign Languages, and the American Studies and Research Center, one of the finest libraries for American literature east of the Suez. During a trip to Calcutta, I had the good fortune of being invited to lecture at Presidency College, one of the nation's premier educational establishments. I was appointed as an examiner for the General English paper of the Central Services exam conducted annually by the Union Public Service Commission. Examiners met in Delhi once a year in order to bring their grading in line with the norms established by the Commission, and this was another opportunity to get to meet English college and university teachers from all over the country. It also gave me a chance to read English being written by students, not necessarily those who had majored in the subject, from all over the country. I remember that one year I graded papers from the South, another year from Gujarat and Rajasthan, and yet another year from north India. I realized that the general level of English was low. Though quite a few examinees had something to say, they were not able to express themselves clearly or correctly, Clichés, unidiomatic expressions, grammatical errors, a wrong use of articles, and spelling mistakes abounded. I began to consider myself fortunate that, whether in Agra or in Delhi or in Shillong, I had had students most of whom wrote better than that.

I had always considered a study of English literature as having played a central role in the formation of my value system, and I had always professed the discipline on the assumption that it was of significance to the lives of the students who studied it. This attitude received a rude shock when my wife and I were invited, sometime in 1977, to a small town in Upper Assam to visit a student who, having just completed his degree at NEHU, had taken up a lectureship at a local college there. It is a beautiful part of the world and we fell in love with it. But the next day, when at his urging we sat in on our student's class, it became clear that though he was undisputedly good, he was failing to relate to his students. He was engaged in teaching Eliot's poetry. He perorated at length about the dissonance in the self that has been caused by the pressures of modern society. But even as he did so, all of us looked out of the big windows on to the lush green paddy fields, the cows being led gently and slowly by the cowherd, the occasional elephant lumbering past, and the alienation from the self seemed to be an unknown disease afflicting people who inhabited another planet. Surrounded by the rustic beauty of Assam, the lament of the woman who, on the sands of Margate, can connect nothing with nothing made no sense whatsoever: it was not anything with which students in the classroom could connect or wanted to connect. Eliot was wasted on them, and I began to recognize that a study of English was not for everyone, nor could it do everybody good. These students should perhaps have been studying Assamese literature instead, or at any rate reading poetry that was far more meaningful to their lives than Eliot would ever be. Was professing English in Shillong doing the inhabitants of the area a service? Or was it a disservice, something that would render them uncomfortable and dissatisfied with their own milieu while not quite making them ready for any other? And even assuming that they could fit into another world, should it be considered a service that they had been plucked out of their quiet, idyllic world and placed into another, more hostile, more alienating, more ugly and corrupt? For the first time I began to entertain serious doubts about the value of what I was engaged in teaching.

I was also beginning to feel a little restless. I was teaching as well as I could; I did not see any way of improving further until and unless the whole structure of teaching and exams was changed. And that was clearly not going to happen. We had hit upon a syllabus which was somewhat like that of Delhi and probably other Indian universities, and everyone seemed quite content with it. We had also, by now, become established inhabitants of Shillong. The place had no surprises for us any more; it seemed that there was little more left to discover. Teaching the students remained a pleasurable activity, but the tensions between me, George, Hom Chaudhuri, and sometimes Anjana Desai, took some of the joy out of the experience.

It was in this mood that I opened a letter one day from Professor A.N. Kaul, the Head of the English Department in Delhi, and a man I had always regarded as a friend and mentor. He asked whether I would like to return to Delhi as a Reader. If I said yes, the post was mine. No interview would be necessary. The invitation came just as I was beginning to tire of Shillong and the affairs of the English Department there. I showed the letter to Frances. She was of the same view as me. It did not take me long to send my assent to Professor Kaul.

I informed the department I was leaving, handed my resignation to the university, and made preparations for my departure. I do not remember any fond farewells or lingering goodbyes or any great expressions of regret. I think people understood that the affairs of the university would soon cause other people to leave as well, and that I was lucky to be getting away when I was. I had helped set the department up on a fairly sound footing, and there was no need for tears at my departure.

Chapter 7
Respice: Looking Back 40+ Years Later

So I returned to Delhi in July 1978 and started teaching at Delhi University; Frances followed the following month and got a job at Miranda House. She did not come alone, for accompanying her was Dolcy Suting, our *kong* from Shillong. We had got permission from her parents to take her to Delhi with us on one condition. They wanted us to ensure that she went to church every Sunday. We were scrupulous in honoring our promise. Her church met at the Imperial Hotel in Connaught Place, and every Sunday Frances and I would escort her there and then bring her back till she had learned her way around and felt confident enough taking the bus unattended both ways. In 1980 our son Virendra ("Viru") was born. He has Down Syndrome, and required special care when a baby. Dolcy became his second mother. She devoted herself wholeheartedly to looking after us, taking care of the house, and minding Viru. There were times when both Frances and I, together with Viru, were away in the United States for months. But Dolcy managed the house, kept accounts scrupulously, paid the bills, and did everything so well that we had no problems whatsoever entrusting our whole lives to her. In 1983 it became necessary for Frances to return to the US on the death of both her parents, and I followed suit in 85. Through lawyers Frances was able to get Dolcy a visa; and, the month before I left India, I put her on the plane for New York. When I arrived, I found that she had settled down quite nicely. Over time she became totally at home in America. She learned to drive, got a license, and became an American citizen. In 2001, when Viru turned 21, she decided to move to Montana where a schoolmate of hers was living; shortly thereafter she met a rancher who was also a farmer and diesel mechanic, and they got married. We were present for the occasion and Viru and I gave the bride away. Though we are separated by 2000 miles, we keep in regular touch by phone, and they visit us when they can, as do we. Dolcy is a very dear and valued member of our family.

She was not the only sentient being that Frances brought with her. There was also Cat. He had had a wonderful time in Shillong. In no time at all he had got completely acclimatized. He would go out and come in through the kitchen window at will, roam all over the place, and on cold winter nights burrow into our beds and sleep at our feet. It was good to see him again, though when he came out of his basket in Delhi he looked bedraggled and lost and confused.

Seeing an open window, he jumped right out. We were somewhat apprehensive, but knowing how he had been able hitherto to find his way back unerringly hoped that he would do the same this time too.

At about 4 o'clock the next morning we were awakened by a loud knocking at the door of our upstairs apartment. The landlord was standing there to announce that a dam had been breached and flood waters were entering our locality. I looked out to see a thin film of water on the street; by six or seven it had swollen to four feet. Clearly our dear Cat had been caught in the flood waters and drowned. Once the waters subsided in a week's time we looked high and low in the hope that he had found a dry spot, but could find no signs of him. We sorrowed for him, but there was nothing we could do. He had been a beloved pet all the time we lived in Shillong, and he came back to Delhi only to die.

Between died a few years after we left Shillong, and the news caused us much grief. She was still young, but I understand that after we left she had had a number of children which left her very weak.

In 1984 I was appointed a full professor of English and in charge of the department at the South Campus. At the interview for this position another candidate was A.G. George. I must say that I enjoyed a little bit of satisfaction and a sense of a wrong being righted in the fact that I got the job and he didn't. I lost contact with him thereafter, but heard once from Noorul Hasan that he had moved to Nagaland, and later on that he had died. But I don't know any details.

Noorul also informed me that Hom Chaudhuri had developed dementia and had to be kept under restraint by his family. I was very sorry to hear this, but again I have no further details.

Temsula Ao, I gather, became Dean of NEHU's Arts Faculty, a short story writer, and was awarded a Padma Shri, news which made me glad. She is retired now, and presumably lives in Nagaland.

The other Naga of the department, Paul Pimomo, came to the University of Southern Illinois to do a Ph.D. We spent a delightful couple of days with him and his family in 1986, when we were driving through. We have kept in sporadic touch ever since. He became a professor at the University of Central Washington, and traveled a bit in Japan and other countries in the far east to lecture there. We met him again when we were visiting Washington State in 2006. He was well settled, his daughter was married, his wife was working, and he was known, loved and respected in his small town where most young men and women seem to have been his students at one time or another.

Noorul wrote a brilliant dissertation on Thomas Hardy at Manchester which was later published as a book. When we stayed with him in 1990 he had become a full professor and was also the Head of the Department at NEHU. I have a photograph somewhere of him sitting at the desk that used to be Dr. George's, with a photograph of W.H. Auden on the wall behind him. His youngest daughter Bulbul, who was born after we left Shillong and is Viru's age, worked as a Montessori teacher in New York and New Jersey for three years, from 2008 to 2011, and lived with us for one of those years. Noorul and I would exchange an occasional email. I was deeply grieved when he passed away a little over a year ago. He was a good friend, and I miss him. His second child Anjum has become quite a well-known writer in India, and her book *The Cosmopolitans* has come in for much praise. We met her some years ago when she was visiting New York, and I saw her again in India when I was there in the winter of 2018.

Prabhu Guptara went to Scotland to do a Ph.D. at Stirling University. He also married an Englishwoman whom he had met in India through their common interest in the study of the Bible. They have four children; two of them, twins, have become quite well-known authors of young adult fiction. Prabhu himself has published quite a bit, including a fair amount of poetry. For many years he worked in Switzerland as an advisor and consultant and traveled extensively over much of the world. Sadly, his wife died after a valiant battle with cancer. He is now retired, has made a home for himself in England, and has just started a publishing house. We keep in touch, and I spent a most pleasant week in his company in London last January. I've always thought it serendipitous that just

as Noorul's two youngest children are twins, so are
two of Prabhu's, and just as his twins have earned a
name for themselves as writers, so has one of Noorul's
daughters. Noorul and Prabhu were the first two
faculty members appointed by NEHU, and the parallel
careers of their children have been interesting to
contemplate.

I lost all contact with Shekhar Singh after we left
Shillong. I believe he returned to Delhi after some
years and got married to Uma Bordoloi, a strikingly
good looking and very cultured, pleasant young
woman who lived with her grandfather just across
the street from us when we moved into Arden, whom
we saw quite a lot of, who became our student in the
M.A. English class, and who acted the part of the first
woman in *Sakharam Binder* opposite me. I have not
met her since leaving Shillong, but understand that
she worked for Air India as a flight attendant, and
now teaches dance at the Sri Ram School for Girls
in Gurgaon, where she is highly regarded. My niece
works in the same school, and through her I was able
to speak to Uma on the phone when I was in Delhi
some years ago.

With the Miris, too, I had no contact till recently,
when through an email I learned that Mrinal had just
had Covid and was still dealing with its adverse side
effects. I understand that he has done well for himself.
From NEHU he went to the Institute for Advanced
Study at Simla as director, and then served as Vice

Chancellor of NEHU—quite a homecoming. He was also a nominated member of the Rajya Sabha, and was awarded a Padma Bhushan.

Towcchaung was transferred to some office in Delhi, and he died a number of years ago. In 2009 we were staying with a grandniece in Sujan Singh Park, and I heard from someone at the India International Center which we were visiting that one of Towchhaung's daughters, who worked at the Center, lived in the Park too. So we dropped in, and were welcomed by the family, including Mrs. Towcchaung. It was a pleasant hour that we spent there.

Dr. Devanesen returned to Madras not long after we left, and died shortly thereafter. We saw the news in *The Times of India*, and I wrote a letter of condolence to Mrs. Devanesen. In her reply she said that her husband had always wanted me to have a professorship. Coming as it did from her, I could not disbelieve it, though I had seen no evidence whatsoever of his wish. Maybe she was just being polite.

So much for the *kongs* and other people in NEHU who find a mention in this book and about whom we know something, however little, from later years. But we knew other people too, not associated with NEHU. What of them?

The most important were Mr. Booth, Mr. Rustomji., the Duaras, and Brendan McCartheigh. In the late 1980s, when we were in New York, Frances woke up in the middle of one night and said that she thought Mr.

Booth had died. It must have been a form of telepathy or some other mode of supernal communication, for we learned afterwards that he had indeed died around that time. He used to say that his ancestor was an Englishman, and that he had American connections too. When we were in Salt Lake City once in the early 1990s, Frances ascertained from the great genealogical records of the Mormons that the family of the Booths was indeed a British family, one branch of which migrated to the United States, and produced both the famous Shakespearean actor Edwin Booth and the notorious assassin of President Abraham Lincoln John Wilkes Booth. Another scion of the family came to India as a soldier. Originally stationed in the plains of what is now Uttar Pradesh, he moved east with the army and ended his career in Assam where he married a Prussian lady. Mr. Booth was a descendant.

Mr. Booth had a number of children. A daughter, Helen, had moved away and we never met her. Ruth and Esther lived with their father. Esther was a student of ours and later worked as a news reader on the Shillong station of All India Radio. Mr. Booth wanted her to have a wider experience of life than Shillong offered and sent her on a trip to England once, but she clearly did not like it and was glad to get back home. I understand that she is no more now. Ruth looked after her father's property after his death; I have no idea what became of her. Mr. Booth

also had a son, Don, who used to drive him around.
He too, I am told, is dead.

After Mr. Rustomji retired, the family moved to
Bombay with which he had always maintained a family
connection. He passed away there a number of years
ago. Some time after that Mrs. Rustomji happened to
be in the United States visiting their daughter, and she
wrote a very kind letter to me. But it happened that
we were in India at the time and did not receive her
letter till we returned to New York, by which time she
had gone back to Bombay. I did not have her Indian
address; and in those days, when Google and other
search engines were not known or else in their infancy,
it was not possible to retrieve it. Therefore I left her
letter unanswered, a regret I have till this day.

The Duaras, too, sold their lovely house in Shillong
and moved to Bombay, where Bapu passed away. I met
Mrs. Duara at a party once in Delhi. It was very good
to see her again, but she was ailing and unhappy, and I
understand that she did not live long after that.

We visited Swarup Mukherji in 1990 when we went
to Shillong, and it was good to catch up with him. He
was his usual witty self, and a great conversationalist,
but he was sick and weak and had given up Cafe Simrit.
I imagine that he must be gone too by now.

Brendan, I am glad to say, is still with us. After
we left Shillong he, too, was transferred by his Order
to various other places, but now lives in Calcutta
where he works with young people who are under

psychological or other kinds of stress. He has set up a hot line for those who may be contemplating suicide so that they may speak to an older, balanced and truly understanding person and receive help. He used to bring out an occasional newsletter which he would send us to keep us up to date on his work. Several years ago he spent a year teaching in Iona College just outside New York which is also run by the Christian Brothers. We would see him when we could, have him over for a meal, and then drive him back. One term Frances, who was serving as the director of our college's English as a Second Language program, needed to hire a faculty member at short notice, and with his Order's permission he taught as our colleague for a semester. He clearly enjoyed New York, but is totally committed to India.

I should say a word here about Lalchand whom I have not mentioned anywhere in the book. He was the first person that Noorul introduced us to when we arrived in Shillong, and Lalchand, in his usual generous manner, invited us to dinner. Through his conversation that evening and from Noorul later on we learned several details about him. He was a Punjabi businessman who had lived in Shillong for many years. He himself said that he was rich, and in 1974 had 86 lakh rupees in his account. He had been married to a Khasi lady but was now divorced, and did not go anywhere without his lawyer because she was doing her best to get her hands on his money. He had two children to whom he was devoted. The son was away studying in Madras, while the girl was a student in Shillong. He had the most phenomenal memory for dates. He could tell you that a certain event occurred on 22 July, which was a Wednesday, or someone said something to him on Tuesday the 3rd. of February. We liked Lalchand but never really became friends; he remained, at best, an acquaintance.

Therefore, several years later, when we were living in Delhi, I was rather surprised to find him at our doorstep one morning. Apparently he had come to Delhi on business and had got our address from Noorul. We were glad to see him and invited him in for breakfast. While we were on our coffees he asked whether we owned the house we were living in. No, I answered, we had taken it on rent. We did not have enough money even to put a down payment on a flat.

Two days later a gentleman I had never met came to see me. He said that he was a business partner of Lalchand, and on Lalchand's instructions had brought a lakh and a half of rupees so that we could put a down payment on an apartment. I was taken aback. Here was Lalchand, a man I knew only casually, advancing a lot of money with no guarantees required, no questions asked, the loan to be paid back as and when I could. It was an incredible act of generosity and kindness. We could not accept the money, though we asked the gentleman to convey our most profound thanks to Lalchand. Though he was only an acquaintance, I remember Lalchand as the most generous man I have known.

John Roche developed a serious heart problem which was responsible for his death in the late 1990s. Towards the end of his life he had started living with a woman, and those were probably the happiest years of his life. I wrote his obituary for the *Record* of our Oxford college.

David Baker and we continue friends, though in his perverse way he has not ever used a computer and so we cannot email. When I saw him in Delhi a couple of years ago, he had aged and was not very well, but he still lives in college and is busily engaged in writing its history. He retains his spark, and his spirit is unbowed.

Tom and Jan Conway lived in Ireland for several years where Jan, now an art historian with specialization in Chinese art, worked at the Chester Beattie Museum. After she retired, they moved to Scotland, where Tom died a couple of years ago at the age of 98. Jan holds the fort valiantly. We stayed with them for a week this past January.

Noreen Dornenberg became an academic after her Ph.D. but gave that up for a career in business. Now retired, she lives outside Pittsburgh. Frances and she keep in very sporadic and infrequent touch.

Vipin Handa joined the Indian Customs Service and did yeoman service stopping smuggling from Pakistan. I was grieved when I heard that he had died in a horrible elevator accident in Delhi.

Rukun worked for the Oxford University Press and published two of my books before setting up as a publisher himself. He has become one of the leading publishers of scholarly books on India under the imprint, Permanent Black, and lives in the hills of Ranikhet, avoiding Delhi as much as he can.

As for us, Viru is now 40 years old, had a part time job in Hostos Community College in the Bronx, our old college which he lost as a result of the Covid pandemic, and lives in a group home under supervised conditions about six miles from us.

Frances and I taught at Hostos, I for 20 years and she for 30. I retired in 2006, and she eight years later. Earlier this year she published her first book, *Scandal and Survival in Nineteenth-Century Scotland, The Life of Jane Cumming,* with Rochester University Press, and remains engaged in various academic projects. I have published five books and various essays on academic or scholarly subjects, but have not done any academic work now for some time. We lead quiet, content lives in a secluded part of New York City, and are happy.

AFTERWORD

*B*ooks speak to us personally, or they don't. This is so especially with memoirs. I read Brijraj Singh's book in just two sittings. Part of my eagerness is attributable to the fact that two of my twelve years in Shillong happened to overlap with the last two of Brij's Four Years in Arden. We were colleagues in the English Department at North-Eastern Hill University in the late 1970s. But it takes a reader more than familiarity with a place and the writer to get as engrossed as I was in Brij's memoir, and it struck me that were I to attempt a memoir of my own on the three-times-the-length of Brij's stay in Shillong, I could end up with one third of his delightful energy and breadth of experiences and possibly a third of his narrative grace. So writing an Afterword, instead, to his immensely rich and fascinating, as well as empathetic and humane, memoir gives me special pleasure.

It is clearly Brij's delightful facility with language that enticed me as a reader in the first place. I find comfort in his well-crafted and spacious sentences. But Brij knows vibrant, smooth language can't do more than invite the reader into his world. So he brews his language, so to speak, with leaven of associative seeing and thinking across the times and the places he knows and writes about so well. He welcomes us to his Four Years in Arden, Shillong, with urbane warmth that his friends know him for and an extraordinary range of local knowledge. And it quickly turns out that what is local to Shillong has a promiscuous evolutionary history familiar in these parts. The indigenous people of the region go back beyond recorded time, they come in contact with colonial Britain in the 19th century, and the contact gives birth to the city that in a matter of decades becomes the political, civil, and educational hub of India's northeastern region.

We know of course that places exist but it is human beings who make histories with places. Shillong offered an exciting setting for making new history with the combined force of human resources on site and an adventurous lot that came, worked, and left or stayed behind. So Brij ferrets out the backstories of notable individuals past and present (late 1970s); he draws our attention to the public institutions that made Shillong what it was then; and he lets us in on the social energies and the cultural life of the city. And he is as good -- even better because of the added humor -- at evoking the daily lives of everyday folk. We get to eavesdrop on him negotiating for the price of pineapples in rudimentary Khasi with local vendors; and Bara Bazaar comes alive in vivid panoramic view on the verbal canvas he paints right in front of our eyes.

It is likely then that most readers of Brij will find something of themselves in this memoir. I can't easily identify what of me is in the book besides the actual reference. My experience of Shillong was unlike his. But I wish I had written about Shillong of the 1970s and the people we shared the city with the way he has in *In Arden*. He writes with the perspective of a man who was placed in a position to interact personally with the governor and the high-end bureaucracy of the state, but who also made the effort to get to know as many people as would allow themselves, and he ventured out to interact with daily wage-earners and villagers. And Brij makes sure that all are spoken for, from the governor down to fruit and fish vendors, with keen fascination and unfailing honesty. Perhaps it is his empathetic temperament and candor, then, that I find myself connecting with most in the book. I find myself included in Brij's empathy with people.

Empathy is also why I was especially moved by sections of the memoir where Brij combines his narrative power of a closely observed event or situation with a transcript of deeply felt reflection prompted by the event. For instance, the unforgettable scene of a dead man on the Baruani train station in the first chapter ends with a brief, seamless meditative excursion within himself on the relative value of human life. Nothing moralistic or philosophical, just a sample of lived interior life engendered by a tragic situation in a familiar public space, what some call "mindful living," which when repeated and extended can help us evolve into our better selves along life's journey, regardless of the places the journey takes us to. This mode of robust mindfulness in everyday living runs through the memoir, so that when we encounter, several chapters into the book, the epitaph on a weatherworn tombstone of "Camilla," the child of a British administrator, we are not surprised by Brij's train of anguished thought on the human story behind the tombstone. Neither are we – readers who know Brij – surprised that he would trace the epitaph to an obscure Milton poem.

So, those of you who may not know Brijraj Singh and have only read about his time in Shillong are probably curious about his life, before and since. You want to get a fuller sense of the man, and I should help you with that. But he can do it better himself, because he has written a book about his calling in life, in *Professing English on Two Continents* (2016). Here's Brijraj Singh in his own words, briefly, about how he got his start in life and the journey that took him to what he calls "professing English":

The son of a loyal and patriotic Indian who served the British Raj selflessly, I was born just before Independence and was therefore a citizen of the Raj, but came to maturity in the years immediately after Independence. Having received a British style Indian public school education, having gone to a school which had an Englishman for principal and his English wife as my most influential teacher, having studied and taught English all my life, having gone to Oxford [as a Rhodes scholar and to Yale on a Fulbright], and later to St. Stephen's which was then perhaps the most "English" institution in all of India, I am, or was, at any rate, more "English" than most of my contemporary Indians. What could be more natural than for me to spend a lifetime professing English?

And Brijraj about himself four decades after he left Shillong:

[H]aving grown up in India, I have never felt anything but Indian. Though I married an American and have lived in the United States for thirty years, I retained my Indian citizenship till nine years ago, and continue to be an Overseas Citizen of India. I don't go to India often, and I know very few Indians in New York, though the city has a large number of them. But I do keep abreast of Indian news and think of India all the time, so that I may be said to inhabit India mentally and emotionally though I live abroad and have few Indian contacts [....]

Just as professing English is no longer professing British literature only, so I cannot see India as merely

India. India has permeated my sense of the West, and the West has permeated my sense of India. For me, teaching, culture, India, America, Britain, the world, Hispanics, African Americans, Chinese, Shakespeare, Rushdie, Marquez: all boundaries have become fluid, interflowing.

All boundaries have become fluid, interflowing. For a person of such sensibilities, we wonder what it means to decide to write a book about Shillong decades after he had left it to continue to profess English elsewhere, in Delhi and New York. It could be that Brij had left something of himself behind, there, or had taken Shillong with him on the journey to wherever he was headed. And so we wonder also if he were to return to Shillong today, would he find in the culture and society of the city something of his idea of professing English that allows for fluid connections across boundaries? How much of his empathetic cosmopolitan self and values would he find there?

Social scientists specializing in the study of the Northeast have tried to find a way to describe the collective storyline of the extremely diverse region that consists of eight states, 101 scheduled tribes, 114 languages, and a population close to 50 million. They see the region as caught up in a series of four "ruptures" in its encounters with modernity: Colonization, Rebellion, Leaving the Frontier, Return (Christian Lund, 2016, Duncan McDuie-Ra, 2019). Each of these periods disrupts the familiar and the traditional, challenging the societies in question to recalibrate life on a large scale, including reframing their worldview in response to the fast-paced, unavoidable changes happening around them, and forcing them to develop new structures of thinking and feeling to deal with the new realities.

Today, Khasi and Jaintia people, the two major ethnic groups of Meghalaya, could be seen as experiencing a mid-way between Rebellion and Leaving the Frontier: rebellion against the legacy of colonial domination by outsiders (*dkhars*) and leaving home for greener pastures in mainland India. The youth are venturing out in growing numbers to metropolitan cities in India, and beyond, in search of higher education, employment, better opportunities. Shillong was different in the 1970s. There were only sporadic signs of resistance to mainland Indians and their hold on the state's civil and administrative power. There was even less resistance to non-native professionals who kept the city running, and taught and administered some of the best schools and colleges in the region. Brij's memoir briefly alludes to expressions of discontent among Khasi youth. In hindsight, though, they were the beginnings of what would become, by the 1990s, a politically charged, organized campaign against *dkhars* led by the Khasi Students Union. The success of the campaign to drive out non-locals from Shillong seems to have made the KSU a political powerhouse in today's public affairs of the state.

That is to say, the socio-political boundaries of Shillong forty years after Brij left Shillong are sharply defined and maintained to keep non-natives out. There's nothing "fluid and interflowing" about the ethnic boundaries in 21st century Shillong. It is important to distinguish this kind of xenophobia from rebellion against colonial rule and dismantling its legacies, which is a necessary duty not just of indigenous peoples everywhere but of freedom loving people anywhere, just as a people's movement for the right to self-determination and self-rule is a just and necessary cause for democracy's survival in the world. Xenophobia is, on the other hand, the antithesis of democracy, especially in the increasingly diverse and interconnected world we live in today.

Ethnocentrism and nativism are not unique to Shillong, or to Meghalaya; they prevail to varying degrees in the whole region. The political antecedent of the phenomenon is common knowledge. The paradox of localism and emigration among the indigenous peoples of the region is not a Janus-faced mythology. It has a clear, causal explanation. But the paradox creates a causal effect on Indians of mainland descent who are born and raised in the Northeast and whose world is destabilized by the consciousness of indigenous peoples' rights to their land. Many non-indigenous people are made to feel unwanted in the region, so that even after having struck deep roots going back generations, or having lived their entire lives there, they come to the conclusion "There is nothing for us here" (Anjum Hasan, *Lunatic in My Head*). So, they migrate to mainland India alongside their indigenous peers. But their journey is not leaving home to return to it better-off like the indigenous youths hope to do, but losing home and roots for someplace else to start anew all over. Their chances of finding a better life on the mainland may turn out better than those of their indigenous counterparts, but the loss is more personal, the kind Edward Said speaks of in *Out of Place: A Memoir*: "The great fear is that departure is the state of being abandoned, even if it is you who leave."

Migrations out of the Northeast, whether for greener pastures or from being forced out, are marked by deep emotional affects. One could nuance the affect in each, and say that anxiety is more pronounced in the indigenous migrant while alienation is dominant in the non-indigenous. But both are present in each. All of them experience displacement from the loss of either family roots or traditional community and must find ways to deal with their predicament. In this regard, both migrants are in the same boat – a "boat on land" – to quote the words of Janice Pariat, a writer from Meghalaya.

Brijraj Singh's *In Arden* can serve the purpose of a whole range of readers. It served two of mine. It brought me hours of reading pleasure. And knowing how different Shillong has become from what it was in the 1970s, I've learned to cherish Brij's Shillong for what it was, without sentimentalizing and wishing it was back. And I am delighted that Brij's empathy and integrity in writing, which glow throughout the memoir, are now available to readers not only in Shillong but in all parts of India, and indeed in most parts of the world.

– Paul Pimomo